D0459688

Confessions of a
GUIDETTE

Confessions of a
GUIDETTE

NICOLE "SNOOKI" POLIZZI

G

GALLERY BOOKS

NEW YORK ✳ LONDON ✳ TORONTO ✳ SYDNEY ✳ NEW DELHI

Gallery Books
A Division of Simon & Schuster, Inc.
1230 Avenue of the Americas
New York, NY 10020

First Gallery Books hardcover edition November 2011

GALLERY BOOKS and colophon are registered trademarks of Simon & Schuster, Inc.

For information about special discounts for bulk purchases, please contact Simon & Schuster Special Sales at 1-866-506-1949 or business@simonandschuster.com.

The Simon & Schuster Speakers Bureau can bring authors to your live event. For more information or to book an event contact the Simon & Schuster Speakers Bureau at 1-866-248-3049 or visit our website at www.simonspeakers.com.

Designed by Jaime Putorti

Manufactured in the United States of America

10   9   8   7   6   5   4   3   2   1

Library of Congress Cataloging-in-Publication Data

Polizzi, Nicole.
  Confessions of a guidette / by Nicole "Snooki" Polizzi.
      p. cm.
1. Polizzi, Nicole. 2. Television personalities—United
States—Biography. 3. Young women—Conduct of life. I. Jersey Shore
(Television program) II. Title.
  PN1992.4.P65A3 2011
  791.4502'8092—dc23
  [B]
  2011033843
ISBN 978-1-4516-5711-1
ISBN 978-1-4516-5714-2 (ebook)

Dedicated to

my cats for bein' the best cats, best friends ever,

and Gia for bein' a crazy spoiled brat.

And to fellow guidettes 'n' guidettes-in-training.

It will soon be a guidette world!

Snooki Revolution!

Kissy face!

Acknowledgments

So many people helped make this book possible—fist pumps, bitches!

First, my family, who is more important to me than life, for always supporting me and my nutballz craziness. I love you, Mom and Dad, for being you and always letting me be me. And my cats, Rocky, Tommy, and Vito, for bein' my best friends ever.

Thank you to Team Snooki! Scott Talarico and Danny Mackey, my managers at Neon Entertainment—you guys are my family and you're amazing, and I love you. Thanks for taking care of me and helping me take over the world! Snooki Revolution! Thanks also to my lawyer, Ryan Nord, for having our backs.

Thank you to my fireman gorilla, Bryan Monti, for traveling with me everywhere and taking care of me. You're the greatest ever, love you, bitch!

A special thank-you to Papa Snooks for running NEP Snooki Enterprises (boss status!) and being my #1 guido/road-trip buddy.

Thank you to Scott Miller, my agent at Trident Media Group, for all his hard work and persistence. You rock, Scott!

Special thanks to my editor, Lauren McKenna, whose vision and hard work on this book made it awesome! She gets honorary guidette status!

Thank you to everyone at Gallery Books. Special thanks to Louise Burke and Jen Bergstrom, the publishers, for their support. Thank you to designer Jaime Putorti, who worked a million crazy hours to get the book rockin' guidette style.

A billion thank-yous to my best broads who are always there for me and keep me grounded through the craziness; love you forever, whores! I couldn't do this crazy life without you at my back. And Jionni LaValle, my boo, thank you for being my best friend and my rock. Love you, poops.

Thank you, MTV, and MTV staff Jessica Zalkind, Lauren Zins, Noelle Llewellyn, and Jackie French, and a special shout-out to my Jersey Shore roomies—you guys are my family and I love you and couldn't imagine life without you.

Thank you to Sondra Zaharias at Getty Images for going above and beyond at every stage of this book. Thanks, American Flyer, for the awesome zebra- and leopard-print luggage that I take friggin' everywhere! And also, Leisure Products, Inc., for letting us use the awesome pink tanning bed for our photo shoot. Thanks to everyone who worked on the photo shoot. And thanks to Andrew Griffiths at Splash News.

Big fist pumps to Robyn Post, my collaborator, who did an amazing job getting my ideas and crazy personality onto the page. You rock, girl!

CONTENTS

Introduction   xi

1   How to Be a Guidette   1

2   Snooki Style Revolution   15

3   My Favorite Things   41

4   Reality Star Princess   63

5   My Jet-Set Life   89

6   My Life Is a Party   103

7   Snookin' for Love   123

8   GTL According to Me   137

9   Outside the Spotlight   151

INTRODUCTION

When you're on reality TV, everyone thinks they know you. People see me as America's #1 party girl, someone who just likes to have a good time. Hello, who doesn't—unless you're a friggin' rock! But reality TV isn't normal life. It's your most dysfunctional moments rolled up in a ball. In my case, a friggin' meatball.

But there's a lot more to me than what you see on *Jersey Shore.* And let's be honest, I'm not the type of person who keeps secrets. But you probably didn't know I was a sci-fi nerd. Or that I want to be a wife, a MILF, and take over the world before I'm thirty. Or that I listen to Christmas music when I'm in a bad mood, or that my cat Vito is gay (it's okay, he's out of the closet).

Ew. I sound like a Match.com profile. (Been on there. Creepers. Just sayin'.) So you have to just read the book! I wrote it to give you a peek into my real life as the world's most famous guidette. 'Cause love me or hate me, you gotta admit, no one rocks guidette status like I do. I mean, seriously? Who did John McCain tweet about tanning? And who did Obama mention in public twice, even though he pretended he didn't (c'mon, Obama, we know you like guidos). Just sayin', I'm boss-lady status in the fricken national government.

I think it's because I'm real. I say what's on my mind, I'm always being myself, I do what I want, and I don't care what people think. And, hell yeah, I

try to have a good time wherever I am. That's what it means to be a guidette princess inside and out. So if you want to learn how I rock it, I'm sharing everything. And my life is pretty amazing, but it's me—so, hello, it's also gonna be dysfunctional!

So strap yourself in, bitches! And get ready for the ride, because only the strong survive.

Guidettes have attitude. We're fearless, and we're confident. We're like that tiny Chihuahua with the mani-pedi that gets up in the Rottweiler's face like it's fricken ten feet tall, barking and growling like a crazy bitch. We do things our way, and we stand up for ourselves no matter what scary creature comes charging at us.

Being a guidette has nothing to do with ethnicity. I'm Chilean and my girl JWoww is Irish and Spanish. It's all about how you look and feel. It's a lifestyle. You've got your surfers, your punks, your rockers, your emos, and then you have your guidettes. We were born to be wild (*Rawr!*), we party hard, we're loud, we're dressed to kill, and we're tan.

But you don't want to be just any guidette. You want to stand out poof and heels above the rest. That means being *you*, doing *you*, and workin' it like you friggin' own it. Guidette status, bitches! Now I'm showin' you how I *rock* it.

1

How to Be
A GUIDETTE

HOW TO BE A GUIDETTE:
My Top 25 Rules

Guidettes are born with attitude. It doesn't matter if you're tall, skinny, round, or a Smurf, or what your background is, we put on our bronzer and we fricken rock our princess status. Like get out of our way, we don't care what you think. Unless you're a mirror.

Attitude is Rule #1. Here are twenty-five more rules for being the ultimate guidette.

1. Always be *you*; be real, be dorky, be stupid, be silly. Like, yeah—dance alone on the friggin' boardwalk like a crazy weirdo if that's what you want to do.

2. It's a guidette's job to look 100 percent perfect from head to toe at all times. Hot outfit, sick nails, hair done, and *tan*! Legit, if you go out looking like a rat's ass, you'll run into the hottest gorilla you've ever seen. KEWL!

3. Your hair should make you six inches taller. Like if you're four-nine, you should be five-three. (How do you think I get on roller coasters? That, and wedges.)

4. Be gaudy, but not tacky. Tacky is bright blue leggings and a pink floral shirt (yack!). Gaudy is excessive animal print and an over-the-top guidette. Love!

5. Life revolves around shopping, tanning, gym, sleeping, and clubbing.

6. If you can smell hair gel from a mile away, it signals guido mating season.

7. Friend your mirror. She's your BFF and a hot-ass bitch. Show her your poses, tell her she's hot. Make out with her. She thinks you're freakin' awesome.

8. Guidettes have Dwayne "the Rock" Johnson balls. We rule and we're not afraid of anything. Except hippos. But they're scary creatures.

9. A guidette has to know how to have fun anywhere. Like if you're stuck in a cardboard box, you have to rock it.

10. Know how to kiss. Seriously? You can't be whipping your hair on the dance floor, all sexy and DTS (down to snuggle), and then kiss like a Saint Bernard. That could extinct the whole guidette race.

Even though we're tiny bitches, I don't give a shit, I will fucking attack you like a squirrel monkey.

11. Feel like a diva at all times. Or just rock a tiara.

12. A guidette is always ready to party.

13. Be real. Tell it like it is. Like if I ask a plumber if he shows crack, and he says yes. Kewl.

14. When in doubt, animal print. Seriously. It solves everything.

15. A guidette has to have her hoop earrings, and they have to be big enough to fit a Red Bull through. Forget that saying "The bigger the hoops, the bigger the whore" (some dumb jerk-off made that one up).

16. Guidettes always have straight hair. If we have naturally straight hair, we straighten it. If we have curly hair, we straighten it. If we want our hair curly, we straighten it first.

17. Be tan. Be brown. Be friggin' orange. Be anything other than pale! Especially in the winter when everyone else looks like they died last week.

18. Learn to hold your breath for like five full minutes (per can of hairspray). Unless you can survive chemical exposure.

19. Always stand up for yourself and your girls. There's always some zoo animal ready to attack like it's the freakin' jungle.

20. Less is *not* more. More is more. If you can't be spotted ten miles away from a helicopter with a blind pilot, add some metallic.

21. Always have a mall disguise. They're just cool.

Animal print, metallic, and bling. I'm standin' out.

22. When a guidette hears house music, even if she's in Walmart, she starts fist-pumping like a spaz. It's involuntary.

23. Boss status! People think if you're tan and you have big hair, you're stupid and superficial. Keep thinking it, jerk-off. Next week, you'll be asking me for a raise.

24. Be strong and independent, so you don't need anyone to fall back on for your Gucci (or your Pucci).

25. Prepare to take over the world, bitches!

7 THINGS A GUIDETTE WOULD NEVER DO

1. Call house music "techno." If a guidette calls house *techno*, you're a wannabe, get real, you know nothing.

2. Pay for our own gas if we only have enough money for shoes and hair products.

3. Use a bump it. Two words: *tease brush!*

4. Smile in pictures. Smiling makes you look like a monkey. We rarely show teeth.

5. Count calories. That's what GTL is for. Don't tell me not to eat a fricken cookie.

6. Go out alone. We travel in packs to fend off rhinos.

7. Go out in public without bronzer, concealer, and lipstick. If you see me like that and I'm not running home, get help, I might be dead.

The Guidette Pose

The guidette hot pose is universal. Even my princess Gia knows the pose. (She's a little fame whore.)

KISSY POSE
Blow a kiss or flash a peace sign.

✳ Make sure you have hot lipstick on (definitely pink).

HAND-ON-HIPS POSE
Shoulders back, boobies out, hand on hips, one leg bent (it gives you skinny arms and legs).

✳ Sexy side look (from your good side).

✳ Do your "hot" face.

Boss Gia telling me how to pose.

Guidette Girl Code
MY RULES

Every guidette should know girl code. There's karma in the code. Like you don't let your girls go to the club looking stupid so you look better (like, really? If you can't be diva-status with other gorgeous guidettes around, you ain't no diva, bitch). Girls can be weird. Honestly? It's hard to find true friends who are real and you can trust and are *seriously* happy for your successes. (I feel so lucky for the broads in my life—love you, whores!) The way you know a true friend is she doesn't break girl code. Here are my rules:

1. If you're catty or fake, you're not my friend. The end.

2. If you're gorgeous and tan, you should be nicer to other girls, not meaner. Hello, how would you like to be ugly and pale?

3. Hos before bros. Guys come and go and act like jerk-offs, but your girls are the ones who will be there for you no matter what, holding your hair when you puke, and helping you stalk your crush. Don't bail on your girls when they need you, or if you find a guido. Always make girl time!

4. Obviously, don't date or hook up with your girl's exes, ex-crushes, or guys that treated your BFF like shit, even if he's a juicehead god, and he looks like Paul Walker. Get your own juicehead. Or a vibrator.

5. Stick up for your girls even if you have to kick some Slopappotamus's ass who's ten times your size. But take your earrings off first or you'll lose a friggin ear.

6. Never compete with other girls, tryin' to one-up them and shit. It's catty and it makes the one who's trying to compete look like an idiot. Do *you*!

7. You want your BFFs to look *hot*! Tell them if their makeup is melting off their face, or they're plucking their eyebrows into friggin' oblivion. Karma, bitches!

8. When your girls ask advice, be straight up. You're not a good friend if you just say what they want to hear. Be real!

9. Main rule of girl code: We do stupid shit. Always be there for your friends (even if they fucked up 'cause they didn't listen to your amazing advice).

10. You can tell your friends are real if they're never fake (like acting like someone's your best friend and then talking shit about them, like in *Mean Girls*).

11. Don't let your girls drunk drive, drunk dial, leave a club with random guys, or run around drunk on a beach like a fricken idiot. If Jenni and Deena didn't try to save me the night I got arrested, I could've easily been eaten by a shark. Kewl!

12. Don't talk shit about your girlfriend's guy, unless he's a major asshole (honestly? All guys have jerk-off in them). Otherwise, it'll be crickets.

13. If you and your friend like the same guy, he's off-limits (bitches before bros!).

14. Don't copycat your girls' looks or clothes or anything else. Rock your own.

15. Girl power, bitches!

THE GUIDETTE LAIR

A guidette is like a jungle cat. She prowls out in the wild (the club). Her room is where she gets beauty sleep, gets ready for the hunt, practices dance moves, and plays Angry Birds on her phone.

The Bedroom

Of course you need a bed fit for a princess. I like live in my bed. Sleeping is my favorite activity. I can sleep in this bed like twenty hours straight, especially after a night out with my girls or sleeping in lame hotel beds! I *love* my pink satin comforter (smush material!), and I switch off between zebra- and leopard-print sheets and pillows. Gotta have my Hello Kitty pillow and stuffed cheetah for snuggling. And my cats. Crocadilly's missing from the pic 'cause he was at the cleaners. He had bronzer on from me smushing him.

On my nightstand I have a leopard-print scarf, zebra lamp, picture of Rocky my kitty, and my Hello Kitty things. I mix leopard and zebra prints because you gotta have *gaudy*. It's like a guidette cocktail.

Dance party! My stereo stand has perfumes on the top shelf, CDs on the second shelf, radio on the third shelf, alcohol and shot glasses on the bottom. Zebra- and leopard-print scarves so you can't mistake it's definitely *my* room!

If I could strap my bed to my ass and take it everywhere, I would.

My Pimp Room (the Bathroom)

I have to keep my pimp room organized. I'm in here half my life 'cause this is where it all goes down, it's where I morph from girl from Poughkeepsie to diva. A carpenter has his workshop, this is my pimpshop. I got all my pimptools set up perfectly 'cause, seriously, what if I get called for a club emergency? I got my basket of eyelashes, basket of bronzer, hairspray, and makeup, and my zebra blow-dryer and straightener. And I don't leave until every one of these friggin' things is on my head somewhere.

The Snictionary

I make up my own words for things (like calling guys gorillas and apes) or my own sounds (*meh!*) or intials (DTS). So here's a guide to the ones I use in this book, plus some that I didn't make up but I say all the time. *Meh!*

Ape—Musclely gorilla over the age of thirty (Roger).

Boss status—You're born a boss. You're independent, you run shit, you get it done, and you own it.

Chode—A guy grenade. Like fat, hairy, and pale.

Crickets—Awkward!

DQ—Drama Queen (What Jionni calls me. Kewl!) Like "You're being a DQ."

DTS—Down to snuggle.

Dysfunctional—If you look it up in the dictionary, you'll see a picture of me and my roomies.

FML—Fuck my life.

Gorilla—A guido juicehead with muscles.

Gorilla central—Heaven! Gorillas all over the place.

Grenade grundle chode—A chode times ten. Like you couldn't pay me enough money to sleep with you.

I hate you, bitch—I love you, whore.

Jiminy/Jiminy Crickets—Awkward times ten.

Jiminy x 10—Off-the-fricken-charts awkward! Like Omg, FML.

Kewl—Sarcastic, when things aren't going your way. As in "I just got a ticket, kewl."

Kooka—Vagina.

Loosey-goose—Like you hook up with too many guys and you're a whore.

Meh—A crazy outburst. Like me and Ryder, every time we see each other, we scream, *"Meh!"*

RNB—Rude nasty bitch.

Snookin' for—On a serious mission.

Snook the night—Party your ass off. From the night I was doing back handsprings with my kookah sticking out at the club.

Team Meatball—Me and Deena. When Team Meatball's here, the party's here!

Tree-branchin'—My favorite dance move. Your arms are stretched out like tree branches swaying in the wind, and you take up the whole friggin' dance floor.

Wah!—Obnoxiously sad or disappointed.

Weh—Cool.

Welp—When you're like "oh well." For example, I'm hungover so I pour a glass of wine. "*Welp!*"

Whatchya gonna do?—Example: "You kissed a 60-year-old man last night." Response: "Welp, whatchya gonna do?"

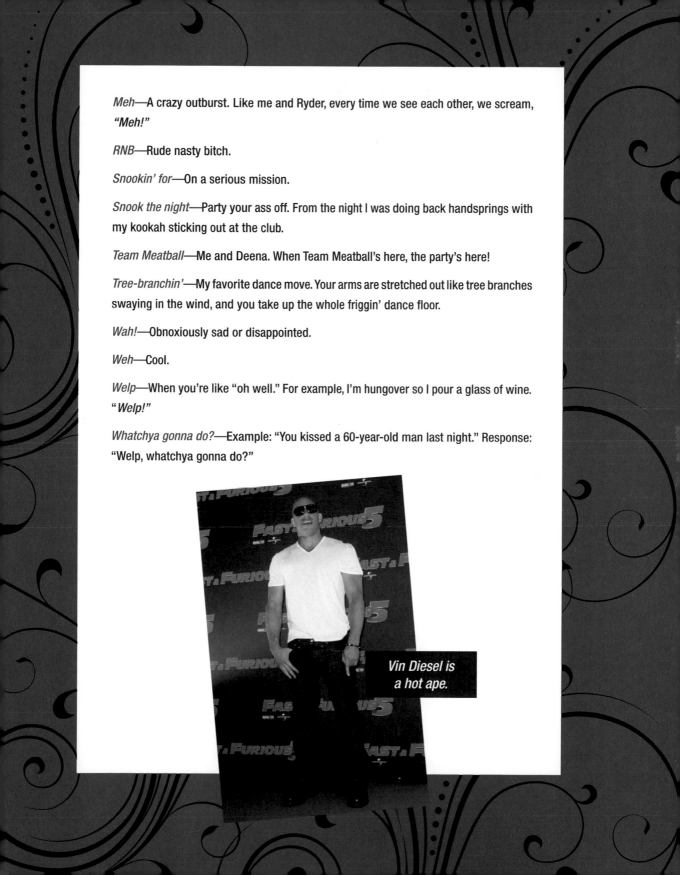

Vin Diesel is a hot ape.

2
Snooki Style
REVOLUTION

Calling all poofheads! Your mission should you choose to accept it is to arm yourself with your bronzer, tease comb, and makeup brushes. We're taking over the world.

It's a Snooki Revolution, bitches!

When guidettes march in, people notice. We have attitude. We're bold. We're sexy. We're tan. And we're causing a serious world shortage of hairspray.

POOF NATION

The Poof Never Dies

If my poof could talk, it would be a badass bitch. It wouldn't take shit from anyone. It would have its own sexy guido gorilla blowout for a boyfriend. It would get invited to the hottest parties.

I'm the only one who can rock the poof without effort. I whip it up in two seconds, and it's done. Perfect. My poof is my signature. And it makes me taller.

I have a love-hate relationship with my poof. When it got famous, and everyone expected me to wear it 24-7, which, honestly, was annoying because I've been wearing it since before Justin Bieber was born, I got bored. I wanted something different. So I started cheating on my poof, rocking other styles, and all of a sudden people went crazy. It was like Brad Pitt left Angelina or something. It was like a national emergency. I started seriously resenting my poof, and I even ignored her.

Of course I missed her after a little while. And she missed me. So we smushed, and then I rocked her again. I'll never stop playing with colors and styles. But I'll always go back to my poof and rock her even bigger. I did my biggest poof ever for *Regis and Kelly.* I almost didn't fit in the door. I wore a sick dress, too.

My biggest nightmare is waking up pale.
Or without eyelashes.

When it's hot, my poof gets exhausted.

Poof Nation!

I invented the poof, bitches.

Waving, Streaking, and Banging It. My Favorite Sick Hairstyles

You have to experiment in life or you're boring. And boring people don't get noticed. Yeah, guidettes like long hair, but you can switch it up in so many fun ways. I put cheetah streaks in, I curl it, I make it black, pink, red. And, no, I don't wear extensions, but thank you hippos on the show for thinking I did and trying to rip them out, that friggin' hurt! The only time I ever wore extensions was for Italy. I wore extensions for Italy when I got leopard ones, and guess what? It friggin' hurts when they put them in! I only wear extensions for color. Don't want to bleach my hair and have it fall out like I'm ninety. I'm totally into headbands right now—fat ones or skinny ones that you can wear across your forehead. All I need is a feather sticking up. I could be Snookahontas. I'd make a hot Indian.

One tip: I keep long bangs because you can wear them down or hide them. Options.

My Kim K hair!

Deep Thoughts

THOUGHTS FROM THE POOF

* "I wonder if Peter Griffin thinks I'm hot."

* "When am I getting abducted again?"

* "My future bedroom: Black carpet. Animal print everywhere. Very gaudy."

* "Would Quagmire go 'Giggity giggity' if he met me?"

* "If I were an avatar, my dragon would be named Tony, and he'd have a blowout and play house music out of his ears and I'd ride him to the tanning salon."

* "Did anyone ever notice that big hair equals genius? Einstein, Malcolm Gladwell, Snooki!

I think she's going to take over the world. . . . Everybody has been really underestimating her. . . . You don't know what's going on in that poof. She could be hiding . . . genius."

—Nicole Richie, *Vanity Fair*

LOOKING SMUSHABLE
My Makeup and Skin Secrets

Why Orange You Tan?

Someone tweeted that I looked pale. Omigod. Biggest. Insult. Ever! And it's not even possible. Tan is my friggin' ethnicity. I'm like multilayered. I have dark Chilean skin, and on top of that I use spray tan, and on top of that the darkest bronzer I can friggin' find. I don't play games with my tan.

I feel like if everyone were tan, there would be no more wars. People would be too busy kissing their reflections in the mirror. (Like we did every time we passed a mirror on *Jersey Shore*.)

McCain would never put a ten percent tax on tanning 'cause he's pale and would probably want to be tan. Obama doesn't have that problem, obviously.

Did you ever see the episode of *Family Guy* (my fave show ever!) where Stewie starts tanning and suddenly he has hot friends and

> Wah! *I'm another race!*
> *But it's better than being pale!*

throws a tan-people party and starts driving a Cadillac toy car? My point exactly! The tanner you are, the hotter you are. And the hotter you are, the *cooler* you are. You don't want to look like a pale vampire. I don't care how hot everyone thinks Edward Cullen is, the boy could use a tan. And I don't care if you're tan from a bottle or spray or whether you're brown or Oompa-Loompa status, just be friggin' tan!

Makeup: Go Mad Hoard

If a guidette is stranded on a desert island, she doesn't need food or water. All she needs is bronzer, pink lipstick, and eyeliner. (Some island guido will get her food and water.)

You're probably thinking, "Why would she need bronzer on an island when she can just get tan?" A guidette can't live on sun alone (besides, you don't want friggin' cancer). We're hoarders. We need our bronzer. I have attachment

disorder to my bronzer. If I lose one, I scream bloody murder, even though there's like ten more in my purse.

Pink lipstick, to me, makes everyone look fresher, tanner, and younger. And honestly? Dark lipstick makes you look like the old lady at the makeup counter. When I do photo shoots and they give me dark lipstick, I look like freakin' Grandma Snooks. Wearing *no* lipstick is just tacky. I keep my Lady Gaga lipstick in my boob at all times.

It's guidette code to rock sexy, smoky eyes, thick black eyeliner, and pink lips (the lighter the better). When you look in the mirror and think even *you'd* want to smush you, you're good to go. One thing I can't live without is my bag of eyelashes. Eyelashes can make feety pajamas look hot. It freaks me out when they fall off. They look like giant spiders and scare the fricken shit out of you.

FIST PUMPS FOR MY
FAVORITE BEAUTY
PRODUCTS (UNTIL MY
OWN LINE COMES OUT!)

✳ MAC, NYX, and Physicians
Formula bronzers (the darker
the better!)

✳ Salon Grafix hair products

✳ Aussie hairspray (it holds
good and smells perfume-y)

✳ MAC everything!

Put a Cat's Toilet on Your Face

My girls and I always pass out with our makeup on after a night at the club, so it's good to get facials. If I can't get to a spa, I'll put kitty litter on my face. (Why not? I love kitties.) LMAO. Before you freak out . . . you don't scoop the friggin' litter from under your cat's butt hole! You get clean litter, mix it with hot water, apply it for ten minutes, and your face will be as smooth as a baby's butt, and your pores will love you. If you think it's gross, you probably already had a cat's toilet on your face because it's *the same stuff they use at the spas!* (In Japan they do bird-shit facials—that's freakin' disgusting.)

I look like a pale freak. I feel like Vinny.

Fake Eyelashes

A GIRL'S BEST FRIEND

A guidette and her eyelashes are like a dog and its tail. If you think it's not attached, you'll chase it like a friggin' nut job. I lost my eyelashes in the Pacific Ocean jet-skiing, and I seriously wanted to go on a rescue mission. In the ocean (I have issues).

I go to Sally Beauty Supply and load up on lashes. I buy all different ones. Like I've worn MAC 34, 38; Ardell 103 Black; Ardell 115 (they look like a small animal); Revlon 91196. They always change. Also CVS! I'll always be a convenience store shopper.

WHAT LASHES I WEAR FOR . . .

Sweats, the beach, shopping, house party. Some people like to wear eyelashes that look more natural. Why would I want to look natural? I like drag queen.

The bar, club, a celebrity event, special occasion. That's when it's time to amp it up and double-eyelash it (then it really looks like a small animal). You want your eyes to look amazing. At photo shoots, the makeup artist will go to trim, and I'm like "You crazy, girl?"

Going all out, like for New Year's Eve or my birthday. Same as for a club or celebrity event, but I might wear sequins or stones in them (just don't get 'em in your eyeballs).

An MTV event. Those are my peeps. I'll do three layers of eyelashes for that!

The Grammys or a high-fashion event. I tone it down. You have to be classy. I only wear one layer of lashes. But one long one!

"I don't think you can drive with these because you'll get a ticket."

MY COLORS, MY STYLE, AND HOW MUCH CAN I SHOW?

I want my style to knock people over when I walk toward them. Either knock them over or confuse them. But I definitely want to stand out!

My #1 Obsession—Shopping, Bitches!

It's my Charlie Sheen addiction and it makes me a winner. It gets me in a good-ass mood. Honestly? I think I have a serious problem and need help. I just went shopping online for a whole month and ordered, legit, enough for a whole guidette army. (A guidette army would be so friggin' cool. We'd throw pickle grenades at everyone.)

I'll rock anything from Bebe, Armani Exchange, Ed Hardy, and Juicy Couture. For events, I love dresses by Jovani or Sherri Hill. People try to glam me up, but seriously, my taste doesn't change.

When I do photo shoots, they try to make me over like I'm a circus freak. They'll give me no makeup, red lipstick, no bronzer, slick my hair back into a bun—like a friggin' librarian!—and put me in some crazy dress that goes down to my ankles like a Pilgrim. I'll suck it up unless it happens more than twice a year. Then I make them take my hair down, tease it back up, give me my bronzer and my leopard dress, and then do the shoot. Seriously. My clothes are too awesome. You can keep your friggin' PTA mom clothes.

My Colors

JUNGLE FEVER! I love anything animal print. Legit, I'm obsessed with leopard. It's like the color of the guidette flag. If you don't have a hundred things in leopard, you're not a guidette. Now if I have my leopard-print heels on, watch out, guidos, I'm going through and destroying things like a freakin' tornado.

BLACK AND RED. If I'm not wearing animal print, it's usually black or red. Or both.

METALLIC. I love anything blinged out and glittery. Metallic is bangin'. Except gold. It makes me feel like a stripper. I'm obsessed with studded and spiked clothes and jewelry. They're edgy and different like me.

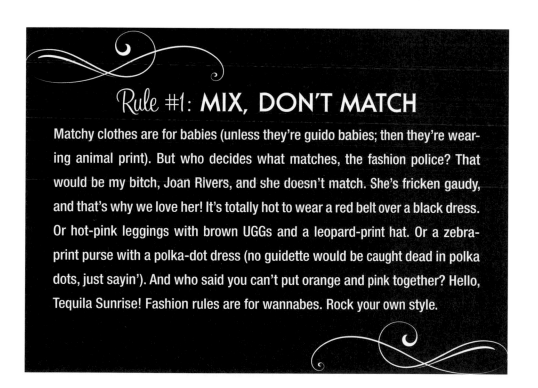

Rule #1: MIX, DON'T MATCH

Matchy clothes are for babies (unless they're guido babies; then they're wearing animal print). But who decides what matches, the fashion police? That would be my bitch, Joan Rivers, and she doesn't match. She's fricken gaudy, and that's why we love her! It's totally hot to wear a red belt over a black dress. Or hot-pink leggings with brown UGGs and a leopard-print hat. Or a zebra-print purse with a polka-dot dress (no guidette would be caught dead in polka dots, just sayin'). And who said you can't put orange and pink together? Hello, Tequila Sunrise! Fashion rules are for wannabes. Rock your own style.

It's my fantasy to smush in a fitting room.

Guidette Must-Have Accessories

Accessories. I like to wear so many accessories that people are confused. My favorites are chunky necklaces that are heavy enough to tow a truck (if they fall into your cleavage, the juiceheads' eyes fall there, too); of course, big-ass hoops; and I love big bracelets or edgy, spiked cuffs on both arms. So if I'm staggering and falling on my face, I'm not drunk, it's just my friggin' accessories.

Hoop earrings tryin' to access another universe—perfect!

Ten pounds of accessories.

Belts. Wide belts give you a waist so you don't look like a stick or a meatball. I wear them over dresses and long tops. They also push your boobs up and out in case you don't have JWoww's balloons of mass destruction. Love that girl's breasts! Just sayin'.

Hate blockers. Sick shades make you look hot, and block the sun, and the haters.

Hats. Everyone looks better in a hat. I like Ed Hardy trucker hats when I'm too lazy to do my hair. Hats are sexy, you can wear them to the club. They're like another hairstyle. I'm officially obsessed with fedoras. (They're my official boss-lady look.)

My hats like to borrow my sunglasses.

My boss-lady hats.

Headbands and hair accessories. I get bored. Things on your head give you something to play with. Plus, you look fricken cute!

Handbags. I change my handbag every two months. They get crusty and rank after that.

My newest obsession.

Butt-crackin' it for the club.

Classy butt crack.

How Much Can I Show?

Let's be honest. I'm not the friggin' Golden Girls.

I LIKE BUTT-CRACK CLEAVAGE. Butt crack makes everything look better.

I LIKE MY DRESSES SHORT. Hi, my name is Nicole, and I'm a dress whore. Seriously. I can't get enough of them. Black dresses, pleather dresses, animal-print dresses. Dresses with feathers. I love anything short and clingy with lots of patterns and blinding metallics. (If you can sit down, it's not tight enough!) The sexier the better. I mean, seriously, what are you, a grandma? Flaunt it! When you're old, you might not wear a dress that almost flashes your kooka, so enjoy it while you can. I go commando a lot, so realize you're commando and hide it like a true guidette soldier. Some girls can rock longer dresses. But I'm four-nine, so if I wore a dress to my knees, I'd have no legs.

My boobs are so tight I can't breathe. Is that normal?

#1 guidette pose.

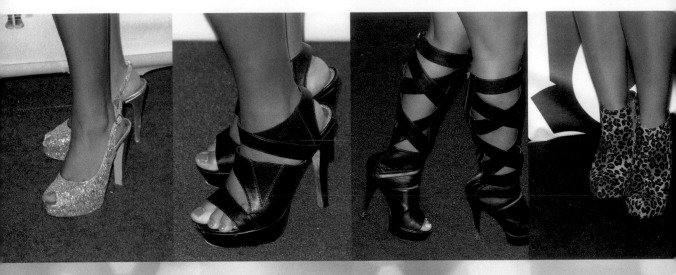

HEELS MAKES YOUR LEGS LOOK LONGER. Rule #1: There's no such thing as too many shoes. Rule #2: Flats are for librarians (unless they're my Snooki slippers, Snooki boots, Snooki flip-flops, or Snooki sandals, LOL!). I'm obsessed with

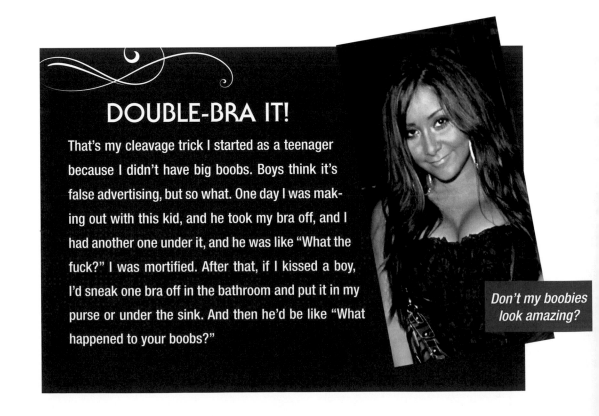

DOUBLE-BRA IT!

That's my cleavage trick I started as a teenager because I didn't have big boobs. Boys think it's false advertising, but so what. One day I was making out with this kid, and he took my bra off, and I had another one under it, and he was like "What the fuck?" I was mortified. After that, if I kissed a boy, I'd sneak one bra off in the bathroom and put it in my purse or under the sink. And then he'd be like "What happened to your boobs?"

Don't my boobies look amazing?

sexy high heels. My favorite shoes *ever* are my Nina Sho-
stoppers that I wore on *David Letterman*; they light up when
you walk. Only someone hot can rock a shoe that lights up
like a friggin' Christmas tree. And of course that's me.

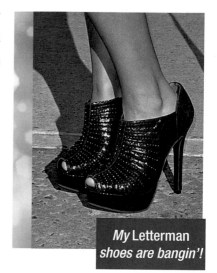

I've got Smurf blood. I've got Smurf feet. I'm a fucking Smurf. So what?

My Letterman
shoes are bangin'!

LEGGINGS. I love leggings! They're better than real pants.
They're skintight, they show curves, and they're hot. If I had to pick one thing
to live in (besides my comfy Hello Kitty pajamas), it would be leggings. Black,
animal print, pink, spandex, whatever. You can dress them up for the club with

some sick heels or wear them with fuzzy boots. But not jeggings. They're wannabes. They're like cucumbers trying to be pickles. Friggin' get over it.

SHORTS OR LONG T-SHIRTS FOR SUMMER, BABY! The shorter the shorts, the longer the legs. Plus, you wouldn't catch a guidette dead in those long surfer shorts. You may as well be a Pilgrim. My favorite thing to wear in summer is a long T-shirt that I wear as a dress. Yeah, your kooka might stick out if you do a faceplant on the beach or a backflip on the boardwalk. (Wear nice underwear just in case! Preferably animal print.)

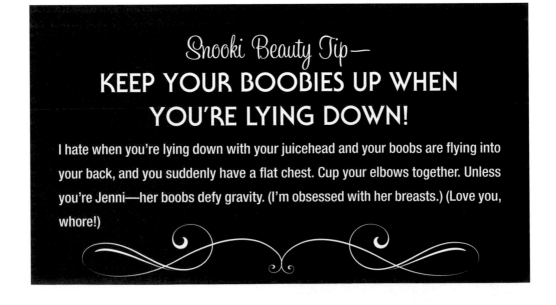

Snooki Beauty Tip—
KEEP YOUR BOOBIES UP WHEN YOU'RE LYING DOWN!

I hate when you're lying down with your juicehead and your boobs are flying into your back, and you suddenly have a flat chest. Cup your elbows together. Unless you're Jenni—her boobs defy gravity. (I'm obsessed with her breasts.) (Love you, whore!)

Every Guidette Outing Is a Party

WHAT TO ROCK

Club. A short, tight dress that shows off legs and butt crack, or something so hot that you stand out; big-ass earrings and lots of bling; four-inch heels *minimum.*

Bar. Black or animal-print leggings or skinny jeans, with four-inch-plus heels or boots, a hot top.

Friend's house. Comfy clothes! Juicy sweats, leggings, shorts, or long T.

Shopping, mani-pedis with the girls. Boots or flip-flops and a kick-ass T. Don't forget the hate blockaz. And eyelashes! Because they make comfy clothes look sexy!

Your birthday party. Something hot to celebrate your bad self. And a tiara. With bling.

SKIRTS: Love them! They make your body look like an hourglass. You can rock a skirt with any shirt and belt.

PANTS: They have to be bleached and ripped or you're a mom.

If I'm not vertically challenged,
I don't know what is . . .
legally, I'm a midget.

ROCKIN' MY SICK NAILS

I love French manicures—they're the guidette default nail. But also rock bling, animal print, and any outrageous design. You gotta do gel or acrylics because when you snook the night, they never fall off.

My Fashion Dos, Don'ts, and Maybes

DOs

The studs will poke your eyes out. Kewl!

When you look like you threw up leopard all over yourself? Guidette heaven!

DON'Ts

First of all, where the hell are my boobs? It's like crouching tiger, hidden boobies! I look like a grandma. The color is boring. I got it at the mall like two hours before the VMAs. Loved the shoes, but my pinkie toe kept popping out the side like the friggin' Whac-A-Mole game on the boardwalk. P-Diddy woulda killed me!

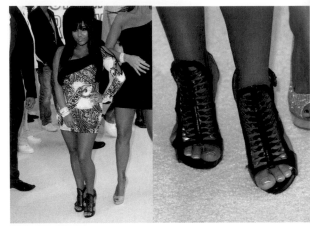

I look like a freakin' blueberry! It makes me want some pie. It also looks like somebody wrapped me in a bandage. Why am I wearing a club dress to the Grammys? And sunglasses from Walgreens. I still rocked it.

What am I, Grandma Snooks the serving wench? I'm like ready for freakin' Oktoberfest. I look elderly and pale! Kewl!

I look like I just landed from Planet Fresh. It's not a dress I'd wear anywhere but the red carpet, but I was rockin' it. Love the metallic. The bracelets were attacking things all night. I wasn't really feeling the grandma orthopedics for shoes.

I liked my Princess Pickle costume, except that I wanted real pickles on the dress and they wouldn't do them! What's a pickle costume without real pickles? Seriously.

Bitch, you fricken stole my look!

3
My Favorite
THINGS

I get obsessed with stuff all the time. I can't help it. I have like an addictive personality. And it could be anything. When I was little, I was obsessed with rocks. Last year, I got completely obsessed with Rihanna and played "Cold Case Love" and "Only Girl (in the World)" over and over in my room like I was stuck in a friggin' time warp. I decided I had a huge girl crush on her and had to go see her in concert like five times. While we were filming *Jersey Shore*, I got obsessed with Jenni's boobs. I love to sleep on them. Better than a temper-pedic pillow. They make everything she puts on look amazing, and I friggin' want a pair. *Wah!*

Sometimes my obsessions are temporary, like Bruno Mars. He's cool, but I'm over it. And sometimes they last—like pickles, or Jenni's boobs. This is just a few of them (I know I need help).

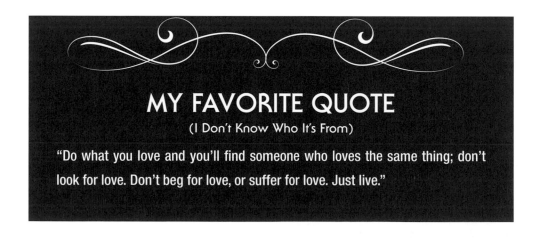

MY FAVORITE QUOTE
(I Don't Know Who It's From)

"Do what you love and you'll find someone who loves the same thing; don't look for love. Don't beg for love, or suffer for love. Just live."

My Snooki Slippers!

Love my Snooki slippers! They're freakin' awesome. I never even wore slippers before *Jersey Shore*. Then I stole Jenni's fuzzy, pink ones in Season One and got addicted. It's like wearing beds on your feet. She bought me green frog slippers in Miami, and I wore them everywhere until they were so disgusting. I wear them out when I'm not in the mood for shoes (hello! Savin' my feet for the ten-inch heels), so I have like twenty pairs. They look like big shoes, they're redic cozy, and they make you taller if you're a Smurf 'cause they have lots of padding. The height made David Letterman dizzy when he tried them on. LMAO.

Hello Kitty

Hello Kitty's my bitch. I love pink and being girlie, and Hello Kitty's so cute and girlie. So what if I'm the only one over twelve that's into Hello Kitty besides Japanese teenagers? (And Josie Stevens, and she's as crazy as I am. Except the girl wanted a Hello Kitty wedding! Love her!) I have like everything Kitty—pil-

low, blanket, pajamas, bathrobe, ring, bling hair clip, brush, picture frame, notepads, tote bag, and phone cover, to name a few. My Hello Kitty stuff plus my leopard-print stuff equals *gaudy.* Purrfect.

Lady Gaga Viva Glam Bright Pink Lipstick

First of all, I'm obsessed with pink lipstick. It makes you look tan and fresh to death. It's like the friggin' guidette anthem for lips. When the Lady Gaga one came out, I was like omigod! I ordered twenty of them, and I still ran out, *Wah!* I also got the MAC Nicki Minaj lipstick, and ran out of that, too, and then they stopped making them (Dear MAC, please keep making these, I fricken need them. Love, Nicole). My backups are MAC Candy Yum-Yum and Behave Yourself. They better not get discontinued! (Mad face.)

I have an addiction to pickles, and shopping, and tan people, and house music, just to name a few.

Blinged-Out Shades

The ones from Miami cost $300. Major rip. I could've bought rhinestones and made them myself for $10. Before we went to Italy, I made my big gorilla fireman friend Bryan go with me to Jo-Ann Fabrics and pick out sequins and glitter and charms so I could make my own (he secretly loved it). I set up shop in my laundry room and was like a friggin' sweatshop in China, pumping out sunglasses. I was like Santa's elves. Check these bitches out. . . .

21 CELEBRITIES I FOLLOW ON TWITTER

My roomies!

Kourtney, Kim, and Khloé Kardashian

Paris and Nicky Hilton

Nicole Richie

Kathy Griffin

Peter Griffin

Snoop Dog

Lady Gaga

Ashton Kutcher

Britney Spears

Christina Aguilera

50 Cent

My Stuffed Animals

I can't sleep without them. Omigod. Just the thought of it gives me an anxiety attack. I slept with a blanket (like Linus), till I was sixteen, then I had to have stuffed animals. They keep away the aliens and the ghosts. Crocadilly's my favorite because he's tall and I sleep with him between my legs, so he goes with me on long trips. But he can't breathe in the suitcase, so I have to carry him. He's my best thing!

An Ode to Pickles

Pickles are like guidos.

Some are green and sour (like after Karma),

Some are limp and mushy,

Some are salty and sweaty (ew!),

Some are cocktail size,

Some are too big and full of themselves.

A fried pickle = tan and juicy.
Husband material, legit.

I smell pickles.

I like to eat my pickles a certain way. I like to suck the juice out first.

I can't see . . . do you have any pickles?

Eating fried pickles was a life-changing experience.

My Phone

I'm obsessed with my phone. I fricken take it to bed with me. If I don't have it for one second, I freak out and panic like a freak. I'm constantly checking it for BBMs (BlackBerry Messenger) and e-mails, reading Google alerts about myself, writing to my Tweedos, or talking to one of my friends. I'm probably gonna BBM or tweet myself to death. I'm serious.

MY TOP 3 TV SHOWS OF ALL TIME

✳ *Family Guy*

✳ *Roswell* (Obsessed!)

✳ *Buffy the Vampire Slayer* (I like the old-school vampires, not the Twilight vampires. Like on *Buffy,* when they turned into vampires, they were the same person. Like Angel was tan. He was a guido vampire. They weren't pale like Edward.)

What I'd Bring to Live on a Desert Island

First of all, I'm not going anywhere without my Hello Kitty pillow, stuffed animals, bronzer, lipstick, and eyeliner. And I have to eat healthy in case a plane filled with guidos crashes on the island. I don't want to be a fat seal barely able to walk.

Broccoli seeds (to plant)

Spinach seeds (to plant)

A shitload of chicken

Hot Pockets (for cheating)

Vodka seltzer

Water

Lemon water

Fuzzy boots

Sexy black heels

Leopard-print dress

Leggings

A hot top that gives me butt crack

iPod with sick beats

Teasing brush

Bows

MY TOP 7 MOVIES OF ALL TIME

❋ *X-Men*

❋ *Avatar*

❋ *Just Married*

❋ *Bring It On*

❋ *A Bronx Tale*

❋ *Selena*

❋ *Titanic* (I know every single line)

Winter

I'm a winter girl. I get so happy in winter. I love the cold and snow and dressing up with leggings and fuzzy boots and going sledding and snowmobiling. And, hello, it's a great excuse to get your guy to cuddle with you and keep you warm under your animal-print comforter!

Christmas

Christmas is my favorite holiday of all time. First of all, it's in the winter, and everyone's happy, families are together, houses are lit up, and presents! What's not to like? Christmas should be once a month. I'm obsessed with Christmas-tree shops—like if I'm in a bad mood, and it's friggin' July, I'll go buy Christmas shit. I watch Christmas movies, and I listen to Christmas music all year. It cheers me up. (*Love* Elvis's "Blue Christmas.") Legit, my iPod's got more Christmas music than house beats.

Firefighters

Love my hot gorillas in uniform! They save people and animals, and they put out fires. I grew up around them; my dad's a volunteer fireman, and we lived in a small town, so lots of people worked at the firehouse, and I used to go play there a lot. Love my boys at the New Yawk Fire Department. We have a family friend who works there. Friggin' gorilla central!

I love my New Yawk firefighters!

Animal Print

I want animal print *everything. Rawr!* My room and my closet look like I threw up leopard and zebra everywhere. I started wearing animal print at like sixteen; it was my guidette coming-out. Like, I'm here, bitches! It's bold, it's hot, it looks good on anything. It's my neutral. I want leopard-print wallpaper. And leopard-print guidos.

I couldn't wait to get an animal-print beanbag. It looks like a pile of cheetah shit.

Rocked this animal-print mani-pedi for Italy.

FAVORITE GAMES TO PLAY ON MY BLACKBERRY/LAPTOP

BOOKWORM. I played this game on a plane to L.A. for like five hours straight. (Come on, worm! You know *GTL* is acceptable, let's be real!) It wouldn't accept *guido* either. WTF?

ANGRY BIRDS. I'm addicted. I got to level four, but I can never kill the green things. They make the weirdest noises.

Tattoos

Tattoos are all-out sexy. Your body's a canvas. Paint some shit on it, and strut it like a friggin' goddess. I got my tramp stamp before I started *Jersey Shore*. It's angel wings with my last name to represent my family, and the wings are people in my family who passed. The second one I've wanted forever and got just before Italy—a rose with rosary beads on my shoulder, because I love roses, and rosary beads remind me of being Catholic, and I'll add my mom's and dad's names in rose petals after they're gone (God forbid!). I got it on my shoulder 'cause I wanted something to show off, and I think it's beautiful! I love tats on guidos. Especially if he's a hot, juicy gorilla, and he has them on his arms, back, or down the side? DTfrigginS!

Boys

Who are these guidos? They're pretty hot.

First of all, who doesn't love boys (unless you're a lesbian). In kindergarten, I wanted to marry them; at twelve, I was the first of my friends to kiss a boy; and in high school, I was friends with more boys than girls because you can trust them more! And, hello, they're sexy and juicy and musclely, and they make you feel safe. And you can cuddle with them, and they keep you warm. And they smell good. And they can pick up shit. And they're hot (except for the ugly ones). I want to live on a desert island with a million guido juiceheads. Just sayin'.

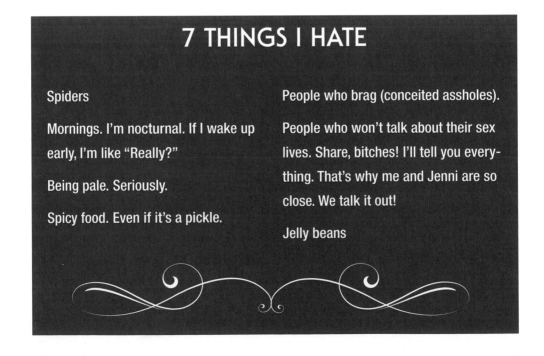

7 THINGS I HATE

Spiders

Mornings. I'm nocturnal. If I wake up early, I'm like "Really?"

Being pale. Seriously.

Spicy food. Even if it's a pickle.

People who brag (conceited assholes).

People who won't talk about their sex lives. Share, bitches! I'll tell you everything. That's why me and Jenni are so close. We talk it out!

Jelly beans

MY OTHER ADDICTIONS

NYPD and FDNY

Shopping

Shopping online
(rehab in my future)

Cats

Johanna from *Real World Austin*

Mob Wives. Me in ten years, minus the mob.

Seriously? When I went shopping in Italy, I needed my suitcase to carry everything I bought. Kewl. I'll check myself into rehab now.

22 THINGS YOU DON'T KNOW ABOUT ME

1. I BOUGHT A TEMPUR-PEDIC MATTRESS. I know it's a grandma bed. But it's friggin' awesome. I put drinks on it and jump up and down, and they don't tip over.

2. I WAS CLASS TREASURER IN SEVENTH GRADE. When you had to do treasurer stuff, like count the money, you had to go downstairs in the basement. So I would take my boyfriend and we'd go down there and make out. My teacher would be like "What took you so long?" And I'd be like "It was a lot of money."

3. I FEEL LIKE I WAS SUPPOSED TO BE BORN IN THE POODLE-SKIRT ERA. Seriously. I love the music and dancing from *Dirty Dancing*. I'd hike the skirt up a little and I'd have a poof instead of a bouff. I'd fit right in.

4. I USED TO COLLECT ROCKS. It started with sedimentary rocks, the ones that are sharp and you can write on concrete and it comes out white like chalk. I'd go to science stores and get the shiny rocks. But that stopped when I started going out with my friends more. I still like rocks. I still have them in my closet.

5. I LIKE STEALING THINGS I WON'T GET ARRESTED FOR. When I was little, I stole shopping bags. I'd play grocery store, and I wanted them crisp so when you opened them, they went phwssht. Then I started stealing coasters. It started with Chili's because they had the Mets on them—I'd go to every table and steal them—then it was Hooters, Ruby Tuesday, everywhere. Now I steal stuff from the hotel minifridge.

6. I SLEEP WITH THE TV ON ALL NIGHT. I'm seriously scared of the dark. At the *Jersey Shore* house there are no TVs and I friggin' hate it! Thank God for Crocadilly. He protects me.

7. I'M SCARED OF THUNDERSTORMS. I have this fear of a tornado coming and I can't get all my cats into the crate to bring them downstairs. They run away from me and I'm like "C'mon, there's a friggin' tornado, we gotta get downstairs!" And they hide under my bed.

8. EVEN IF THERE'S NO THUNDERSTORM, I HAVE TORNADO NIGHTMARES. I've always had dreams that there's a big tornado and then five little ones, and they're just coming straight at me and I hide in the tub.

WHAT'S ON MY IPOD
MY FAVORITE BEATS

Usher, "There Goes My Baby"

Rihanna, "Rockstar 101"

Rihanna, "Cold Case Love"

Soulja Boy, "The Best"

Drake, "My Type"

Those Usual Suspects, "Shadows"

Drake, "9 A.M. in Dallas"

Rihanna, "Tè Amo"

Chris Brown, "Without You"

Dobenbeck, "Please Don't Go"

Dash Berlin, "You and I"

Akon, "Once Radio"

Dubfire vs. EDX, "Final Road"

Kings of Leon, "Use Somebody (Christian Luke ReBoot)" (Wanna play this at my wedding!)

Chris Isaak, "Wicked Game"

Armin Van Buuren, "Drowning (Avicii Mix)"

Kim Sozzi, "Feel Your Love"

Deadmau5, "The Reward is Cheese"

Kreayshawn, "Gucci, Gucci"

9. I'M A CLOSET ALTERNATIVE-ROCK AND COUNTRY-MUSIC FAN. I like Staind, Coldplay, Foo Fighters, and Goo Goo Dolls. But house music is my mating call.

10. I MAKE A WISH WHEN IT'S 11:11 ON THE CLOCK, IF I GO THROUGH A YELLOW LIGHT, OR IF I GO OVER TRAIN TRACKS. I lift my legs up and make a wish. We'll see if Peter Griffin asks me out.

11. I'M REALLY A GEEK. I've seen every sci-fi movie ever made. I own every DVD of *Roswell*. I'm obsessed with movies about humans being aliens. I could be an alien and you wouldn't even know. X-Men! Love!

12. I LOVED ACTING OUT SHAKESPEARE PLAYS IN ENGLISH CLASS. I'd act out all the main characters' parts and do their accents—I'd be Romeo and then do Juliet, and the class would crack up, thank you.

13. WHEN I WAS THIRTEEN, MY WALLS WERE COVERED WITH 'NSYNC PICTURES. Figures my favorite one, Lance Bass, turned out gay. I'd still make out with him.

14. MY MIDDLE NAME IS ELIZABETH. It doesn't even end in a vowel. Jiminy.

15. I HAVE A HIDDEN TALENT. I produce music on my computer. I started off making beats with FruityLoops, which is what DJs and big producers use. But that took me hours, so now I do it on my Mac. I can't read music, but it's like if I hear a beat in my head, I can play it on the piano or drums. In cheerleading, I did all of our mixes for competitions. Move over Pauly D. Snooki P in the house, bitches!

I hate the ocean. It's all whale sperm . . . everybody, google it, because that's why the water's salty. It's fucking whale sperm.

That's why I don't eat lobsters and stuff. Because they're alive when you kill them.

16. I WON'T EAT SOUP UNLESS IT HAS GRATED CHEESE ON TOP.

17. I WON'T EAT *ANYTHING* THAT COMES OUT OF THE OCEAN. Ew. My version of sushi is California rolls.

18. MY DREAM CAR IS AN ESCALADE. Black with rims. But I need a staircase to get in it.

19. SOMETIMES I'D MUCH RATHER STAY IN AND WATCH MOVIES THAN GO TO A CLUB.

20. I WAS AN ALTAR GIRL. But I would make fun of the priest and try to light his hair on fire. (I was like seven.)

21. I DIE LAUGHING WHEN PEOPLE STUB THEIR TOES.

22. I HAVE CRAZY DREAMS. Like I dreamt the world was ending and I was put in a fireproof ball with 50 Cent and Robert De Niro.

OMG, the sky in my area is as black as King Kong's butthole. I don't do storms.

My Perfect Day

Wake up at twelve.

Take one-half hour to get out of bed.

No breakfast. (Unless I won't get to eat for a long time. Then egg whites.)

Gym!

Shopping. (If I ever go to rehab, it will be for shopping.)

Drive around and figure out what my girls are doing.

Nap until nine.

Get ready to go out.

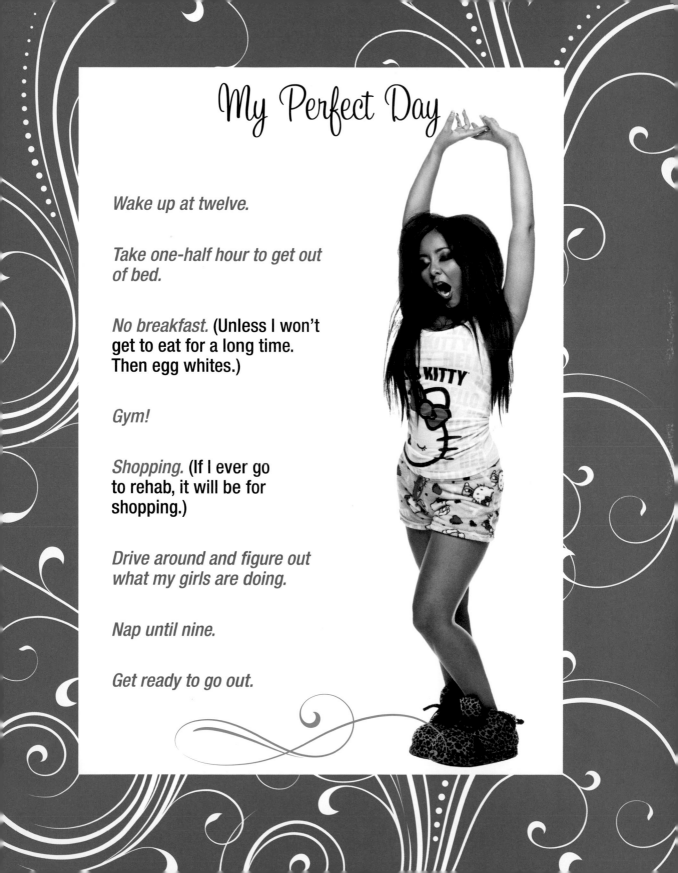

4

Reality Star
PRINCESS

I always wanted to be famous. I don't know why, I just did. When shows like *Real World* came out, I was obsessed. I was like "I like to party, I like drama, I could fit right in." I auditioned for *Is She Really Going Out With Him?* on MTV, about hot girls that date jerk-offs, and got on, but nobody watched it. Then I saw an ad on Facebook that said, "Calling all guidos and guidettes," and I was like, seriously? My friggin' dream job! I happened to be at the Jersey shore and the audition was down the street, so I go down there with my big poof and my ten layers of bronzer, and my fake fur coat, and black leggings and six-inch heels, thinking I'm hot shit because I always think I'm hot shit. They took me down into this creepy fricken cellar, that was all dark and had a camera in the middle, like you're doing a porno. The producer was probably like "What is that?" when they saw me. They probably figured, "She's orange, she's feisty, she says what's on her mind . . . *dramaaaa* . . . we'll take her!" I thought *Jersey Shore* was going to be some other show nobody watched, and then I was at a bar in my hometown and somebody said, "Are you the girl from that show?" And I was like, omigod, somebody's watching it!

It has been balls-to-the-walls insanity since the debut. Honestly? Me and my roomies are so crazy that even the camera crew can't wait to see what happens next. They try to get night shifts because during the day we're boring, but at night we go clubbing and the scary creatures come out.

I am a princess at home,
like I am the fucking princess of fucking
Poughkeepsie. Here I am nobody.
I am emotionally exhausted.

I'm Goin' to the Jersey Shore, Bitch!

When taping started, I went to the house thinking I was just gonna go insane. I'd just broken up with a guy and hadn't been single in five years, and my head was all messed up. I didn't know how to be without a boyfriend. So I went there to have fun, party, and be stupid. When I stepped into the house and met all my roommates, I was like "What? This is the house? Really?" I thought it was going to be some amazing mansion, with sexy, sexy people. So I decided to just get drunk. Then I woke up hungover and sick, upset about my breakup, homesick, and my roommates hated me. I hid in my room for like four days freaking myself out. I was only twenty-one, I always had my parents to coddle me, and I was on my own for the first time, and I wanted to go home. So that's how it all started.

Then you had the cameras. I always liked cameras in my face (I've been downloading YouTube videos of myself since high school!), but to have them follow you around 24-7? You're sitting on the couch and they're taping you sitting on the couch. Crickets! I wanted to say, "Get the hell out of my face, I'm not doing anything, I'm just trying to relax!" People think my roomies and I are crazy, but you're in a house with no TV, Internet, or contact with the outside world except for the freakin' duck phone, with a bunch of weirdos and alcohol, and fifty cameras in every corner. It's not normal! You hear the cameras zooming in and out like aliens, even when you're sleeping. And you don't know who's watching so you get paranoid. We're like a science experiment. When I get home, I have nightmares I'm being watched.

But, honestly, you have your bad days when you want to run the frig away, but you also have days where you love having the cameras in your face (how many people get to do this?), and we have fun, because we're all nut jobs. After a few months of not filming, I can't wait to go back in the house and be with my roomies.

The Jersey Shore House

First of all, the house is a filthbox. There are condoms everywhere. Red plastic cups everywhere. It smells like alcohol and dog's butt. When we cleaned it—we cleaned on Sundays—we'd ruin it again that night. It's a miracle none of us got a disease.

Seasons 1 Through 3: My Narration

SEASON 1: SEASIDE. First day in the house, I go in thinking this is going to be a party, everyone's going to love me—I'm fun, I'm hot, the Jersey shore's been my party place forever (even before alcohol), let's get crazy. But then I get drunk, act trashy, black out, and everyone hates me, because they think I'm a crazy nut job. They didn't even want to get to know me after that. Nice first impression, Nicole. Honestly? Who friggin' blacks out their first day meeting people? Only me. When you black out, you feel like you're abducted by aliens 'cause you don't remember anything. The next day I'll say hi to someone and they're like "Fuck you," and I'm like "Why?" My friends call me Dren from the movie *Splice* 'cause the Dren is this crazy horny alien bitch. So I hid in my bed for like four days, seriously depressed and completely freaked out and missing my family and I decided to go home. But then Sammi gave me a pep talk and I decided to stick it out. I sat everyone down and said, "I feel like shit, can we please start over?"

It was weird and like crickets living in a house with a bunch of people you don't know. What brought us together was when the loser of America punched me in the face. We were all getting along and vibing that night, and the loser came over and was stealing our drinks and I was like "Get your own drinks,"

and next thing I know I'm on the fricken floor. I was so scared and freaked out. My first thought was "If I have no teeth, I'm leaving. I can't do the show with no teeth." But no broken jaw, no broken teeth, I learned I have a hard face. That was the first time we realized we're a family, and I felt like I was part of it, and if you fuck with one of us, you're fucking with all of us. And then everyone in the house started to see I was pretty cool. Me and Jenni started getting close (love you boo boo). Sammi too, but she was always with Ron, and that drama was starting. Angelina leaving was like "Good riddance." She disrupted the house. So it was me and Jenni, we were each other's boos.

First season I snooked for love the whole time, what a waste! There were no good juiceheads in the entire Sleazeside. I thought the boys in the house were cute (and they could cook. Hello, boys that can cook!), but they were sluts. Except Vinny. He was a sweet little mama's boy (but that only lasted one season before Pauly corrupted him!).

SEASON 2 (PART 1): MIAMI. It was weird to film the show anywhere other than the Jersey shore (hello, guido central!), but I couldn't wait to try something different. Miami is all beautiful people and hot clubs. I figured all new guys, not the same ones we always see in Seaside, and they'd be tan and redic hot.

Road-trippin' down me and Jenni were praying Angelina wasn't gonna be there, because first the shit from Season One, and then after filming, she was trash-talking me and Jenni behind our backs. So when we walked in, and she was there, I was like FML, I couldn't even handle it, I had to hide in my fricken room. And then I tried to give her a chance and she hooked up with Vinny after

Watchin' this Jersey Shore *show I heard about.*
What a bunch of orange nut jobs!

I did. Um, no. That's girl code. You don't do that. Fast-forward to kicking her ass (hold my earrings!), the best part of Season Two.

The guy who cheated on me, whose name I won't mention . . . I was a fucking idiot. But I learn from my mistakes. Burning the pictures was good, we did it as a family, and it helped me get over him. After like two weeks Party Snooki was back! The Miami clubs are the hottest clubs in the world. It's like a 24-7 mad, sexy vibe. Seriously, I partied so much it scared me. In Miami you can have a cocktail at ten in the morning and it's normal. In Jersey if you do that, you're an alcoholic. Thank God Team Meatball wasn't there or we'd be dead.

But there were no friggin' guidos in friggin' Miami! Not one freakin' juicehead. I was pretty much hating the entire male race anyway and wanted to turn lesbian. No guidos in the entire state and the boys in the house were being weird. Pauly (my baby's daddy) went from being the quiet one to the loudest in the house, Vinny turned into a pimp, and Mike got weird and turned into a dick.

Me and Jenni got closer in Miami because she was totally there for me. And we were the only girls left since Sammi wasn't talking to us. But no regrets about the latter. We tried to help our girl out—it's girl code, but hello, Ron is one of our roomies too. So that was bad. We were so over their drama. Miami was seriously dysfunctional. It wasn't my favorite season. But the fashion scene was redic, and I shopped too much ($300 blinged-out shades).

SEASON 2 (PART 2): SEASIDE. It was such a relief to be back in Jersey to my own people! Fist-pumping and guidos and jerk-offs. Home sweet home!

And Team Meatball! Deena's gorgeous, she's a sweetheart, she knows how to party, she's just like me. She's like my Ryder in the house, we have a good time in any situation; she made the house fun. But I knew something was gonna go down with Sammi from what happened in Miami. A new person, and we

5 THINGS TO EAT WHEN YOU COME HOME FROM THE CLUB AT 4:00 A.M.

Grilled cheese (duh)

Turkey burgers

Cinnamon Toast Crunch (yum!)

Pizza Bites

Hot dogs

can't be fake in the house. Honestly though? I was so happy when all the girls finally made up with Sammi. I have a hard time being mad at people (unless they do something really bad) and I wanted to make up with her the whole time.

Meanwhile, the boys were ampin' up their game and getting weirder. They were bringing home creatures that looked like they were from *The Hills Have Eyes*.

What happened to Jenni—what Tom did to her—was horrible, I wanted to rip his balls off. I couldn't stand seeing her sad, but she was there for me and I got to be there for her. *Jersey Shore* was the best thing that could've happened to her because it got her away from him. It all turned out good. She got a real gorilla juicehead ape (love you, Roger!) and I got Party Jenni back (pee-behind-the-bar no-boundaries Jenni), and it was on! It was back to snookin' for guidos (fuck the lean cuisines in Miami!). The whole thing where I was DTS with three guys and they ended up knowing each other, that was like "Really?" Obviously I was thinking with my vagina and not my brain. (If you don't remember, watch that episode again. Crazy shit.)

I'm not even gonna comment on Vinny. I liked him, we had a bond, we snuggled, and then he turned into a pimp. The end.

Just like the Ron and Sam drama. That went to a new level of insanity. I love them both, but we were already over it from Season One.

Getting arrested was the worst thing that happened, obviously. I started drinking at like 10:00 a.m. to cure my hangover and woke up in a jail cell. When I watched the show, I was afraid to see what I did, because I was abducted so I didn't know. Honestly, I hate seeing myself like that. I hate it. I'm like "Really, Nicole?" I look like a friggin' alcoholic, I look gross.

I would have thrown me in jail. You can't have this little meatball running around drunk on a family-oriented beach, faceplanting on little kids, and cursing out cops. But jail sucks. It's scary. I'd rather be in a dog pound. I'm too pretty for jail. But I don't regret it. It was a lesson learned.

The best part of Season Two was the pranks. I gotta give it to Mike for the New York prank (even though I wanted to kill him). But when we put the cheese under his mattress, and he thought his girl stunk like cheese, and then we said, "What, you didn't know? Girls smell like that sometimes," and he believed us until the last day at the shore?! Victory, bitches!

SEASON 3: ITALY. Sorry, bitches, you're gonna have to watch to find out (hope you watched already!). As I'm writing this, I can't talk about it yet, but I'll give you my two cents in my next book! Insanity.

My BFFs for Life

My roomies are my best friends. When you have to make your own fun, you either amp it up, go crazy, or kill each other. In one day we could go from "I hate you, I hope you die" to "Omigod, I love you for life," but we're there for each other when it matters. We know how to push each other's buttons, and we know how to friggin' party. We're a weird, dysfunctional family of oddballs. Like the Addams family, except hot.

PAULY. Pauly is a spaz, he like bursts out yelling shit, and you're like omigod. But I want to have baby guidos with him, he's so hot. You can't get mad at him or start a fight because it's like trying to be mad at a puppy. He's like the

class clown. His suitcase is bigger than the girls' when we travel.

VINNY. In one year he went from a nice mama's boy who missed his house and his bed to thinking he was a pimp. It started in Miami when he was hanging out with Pauly. Now he thinks he's the hottest thing to hit the earth. Like a ladies' man. Yeah, Vinny, and then you woke up twice. You need to keep your horse penis to yourself.

MIKE. The boy is obsessed with facial care. He's like one of those little hamsters that stops eating every five seconds to wash his little hamster face. Mike washes his face all day long. He does face masks, and he puts one on me and we do it together like girlfriends.

FOUR THINGS I TRIED
TO HIDE FROM THE CAMERAS

1. My morning face! I'd dodge the cameras and run for the bathroom. Especially after a night at Karma, I looked like a friggin' sewer creature.

2. We'd try to talk shit in the bathroom, but they'd catch us right away.

3. It was impossible to hook up secretly. We gave that up first season.

4. Vibrator time. The only place they didn't follow you was in the shower. That's why we stayed in there for three hours.

We are legit wackadoos.

Wall Street guidos. The stocks went up!

SAMMI. Sammi's a good girlfriend to have. She's a great listener and gives good advice. Nobody would ever know she burps a lot. If you look at her, you'd never expect her to burp, that's why I love her!

RONNIE. He's like a big frat boy who tortures you. Like a big brother. If I hook up with a guy, you know the "walk of shame"? Well, Ronnie makes it ten times worse. He'll be like "Omigod, you slept with him? He's so ugly." And he'll get in your face and laugh like an insane person.

DEENA. Deena's my girl. She's such a weirdo, like me. She sleeps with twenty stuffed animals in her bed. It looks like a Disney castle. It has every stuffed animal you can think of. She's a little kid trapped in a little meatball body.

JENNI. Jenni is my boo. When she wakes up in the morning, her hair is everywhere, and she looks like a crazy homeless person (she's still the cutest thing ever). We'd fight in the morning because some days I'd wake up with my makeup and hair perfect from the night before, and she would call me a friggin' whore. When I sleep, I don't move. I just stay there, and she's all over the place. I'm obsessed with Jenni. I wanted to be her for Halloween. I'm seriously in love with her. And her tatas.

The Next Incarnation of Jersey Shore

We never know if there will be more seasons, but we'll all be going to the Jersey shore anyway, so why not film it? I think we could all keep doing it till we're ninety. Or until our livers give out.

Did you ever see me do my raptor impression from like Jurassic Park? Jenni said it was the creepiest fuckin' thing she's ever seen in her life. I'm good.

Awards for My Roomies

★ *Biggest Fame Whore:* Mike

★ *Biggest Slut:* Mike

★ *Freshest to Death:* Pauly

★ *Most Transformed:* Vinny

★ *Nicest:* Deena

★ *Most Logical:* Jenni and Pauly. Jenni's the oldest girl and Pauly's the oldest guy, so they gave good advice. But we still made asses of ourselves.

★ *Sloppiest:* Me. I'm used to my mom cleaning. *Wah!*

★ *Neatest:* Pauly. He'd be a good househusband.

★ *Best Dancers:* Ronnie and Vinny. They never show us dancing on the show! Boo.

★ *Hogged the Bathroom the Most:* Sam and Mike. Sam straightens her hair for five hours and Mike washes his face for five hours.

★ *Loudest:* Pauly. Omigod. You want to kill him if you're sleeping. But you can't because he's a friggin' puppy dog.

My Fans' Favorite Jersey Shore quotes

If you want me to cook and poison everybody and we're gonna
be dead in two minutes. Whatever.

✳

I can't see any ice creams, I can't see any customers,
'cause I'm a fuckin' Smurf.

✳

We're delicate princesses. You're not supposed to throw water
balloons at us like that!

✳

Get it all out, fricken do everything that you can . . .
have sex with an old man, steal a plant,
and then get arrested, and then do whatever.

✳

I feel like a Pilgrim from the fuckin' twenties washing
shit right now.

TALK SHOWS, AWARD SHOWS, AND WHO'S THE BOSS

Talk Show Queen

I'm like a professional talk show guest now. I've been on every show like ten times. I think they like me because I just say whatever, they never know what's gonna come out of my mouth. And I get to do some crazy shit.

JIMMY KIMMEL. I have a redic crush on the man. He wanted me to put on a Snooki monster costume and I was like "No way, it's not even tan." But then I saw it had a poof, so I was like "Okay, I'll rock it!"

Radio show queen, holla!

DAVID LETTERMAN. On one of his shows I did, I did the Top Ten Reasons to Buy the New Snooki Book. If I got to write it, it would've been *way* funnier. Like, hello, guidos don't drive Camaros, they drive BMWs and Cadillacs. On another show, I got Dave to fist-pump and try on my Snooki slippers. He can't be a guido because guidos aren't named Dave. But he could be an ape.

JIMMY FALLON. He's so funny and cool. He drank pickle shots with me and almost puked pickles. Amateur. (Love you, boo.) Plus, he's from my area! We get each other.

JAY LENO. Chris Rock was on, and when I came out, he said he wasn't familiar with *Jersey Shore*, and I said, "Do you live under a rock?" and Leno said, "His wife does." And I was like "Huh?" Then when I watched it later, I was like "Oh, right, Chris *Rock*. Duh." Still a really bad smush joke, Jay.

My roomies and I were on Barbara Walters's *10 Most Fascinating People of 2010.* That was insane. It was like meeting Elvis. She asked us what *GTL* meant. We need to put some leopard print on her and some six-inch stilettos and take her to Karma. Bet she can kick some elephant ass.

Reality Show Guest

I did an episode of *Cake Boss*. First of all, it's in Hoboken; I've been partying there forever. Meeting Buddy was better than meeting any celebrity. I'm the hugest fan. He made this strawberry-vanilla cake for my mom that was amazing. His pale cousin, who didn't know what *GTL* was, was being a creeper and trying to pick me up. You can tell on the show I'm like "crickets."

Entertainer

Whenever I do appearances at clubs or shows at college campuses, someone always asks me to stand next to them so they can see how short I really am. I'm a Smurf, people. Friggin' get over it!

The Q&A sessions at schools are really fun, but we have to weed out the pervy questions before the show— like how big is Vinny's penis,

or what Disney character would I have sex with. Seriously, people? I love the one-on-one time after my shows. People bring me presents and handwritten cards. I'll walk away with like eight jars of pickles.

One of the most fun things I did this year was *Salute the Troops*. Love the USA and love my gorillas in uniform! To all the military people who serve our country, thank you and I love you, bitches! You're all hot.

MY EVOLUTION TO GUIDETTEHOOD

When I was sixteen, I was a total preppie tomboy. I wore like polo shirts and stuff and was into four-wheeling and snowboarding and being a boy. Then I went to teen night at this dance club called Matrix, and I'm wearing a grandma dress, all covered up, and I see these Long Island girls in skimpy dresses, and they were hot and tan, and they had attitude and big hair. I'd never seen girls like that before. And then I see these hot guidos and I was like "Omigod, this is friggin' amazing!" So I deaded the grandma dresses and became a whore. But I'm still a tomboy.

Grammys, Baby!

MTV News asked me to interview people on the red carpet, and I had no idea what the frig I was doing. I was out there on the carpet going, "Who are you? What do you do?" I met the band Phoenix and they're French, and they didn't know what guidos were and I was trying to explain it, and they were like "Oh, *cagole*!" I think they called me a whore. But I had a blast because

My Grammy partner, Sway, and I doing Sirius radio. We're badass.

I met tons of amazing people that night, like Katy Perry and Fergie, and Miley Cyrus (my bad bitches). The next year, I was prepared: I did some research and I rocked it.

Doin' the MTV Awards!

Bestselling Author

I love making up stories and making people laugh. Every hippo and catfight we had while filming *Jersey Shore* gave me ideas, and I had tons of ideas for characters and drama. I love that I got to do something people didn't expect and they didn't expect it to be so good. *New York Times* bestseller, bitches!

The best part is book signings. I got to be one-on-one with my fans. Little girls would be dressed like me, and people would bring gifts when they got their books signed. They came just to see me, I loved it, it was insane.

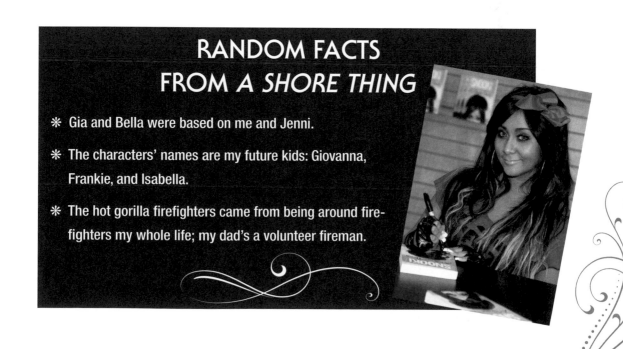

RANDOM FACTS FROM *A SHORE THING*

✳ Gia and Bella were based on me and Jenni.

✳ The characters' names are my future kids: Giovanna, Frankie, and Isabella.

✳ The hot gorilla firefighters came from being around firefighters my whole life; my dad's a volunteer fireman.

Bein' Boss Lady

If you're a guidette, you're boss status. I like bossing people around. LOL. But seriously? I feel like you have to take what you know and run the show. I've gotten smart about business, and I'm trying to brand myself. I want an empire, like Oprah (the girl has big hair and she's tan, just sayin'). I've got my Snooki Slippers, my sunglasses line, my flip-flops, boots, and sandals, and I'm working on perfume and hair and makeup products. I want TV shows. I want it all. It's a Snooki Revolution, bitches! (I just wanna wear killa boss-lady hats.)

A Tribute to Haters

DEFINITION OF A HATER: (1) unhappy person who doesn't like others to succeed; (2) gets off on taking other people down; (3) drinks too much haterade.

When you're popular, you have haters; when you're interesting, you have haters; when you're pretty, you have haters; when you're successful, you have haters.

I wanna tattoo GET OFFA ME on my knuckles so it's the last thing my haters see before I punch them. But let's be real. If you don't have haters, it means you're friggin' boring. Haters only hate if you're doing something great. (Unless you're just a jerk-off.) So I try to embrace my haters. They inspire me to succeed even more.

A Love Letter to My Haters

Dear Haters:

Glad I'm doing something worth your time.

Thanks for caring.

But how 'bout you do you instead.

♥ Love, Nicole

5

My Jet-Set
LIFE

PLANES, TRAINS, AND FRANKIE THE BEEMA

Flying

I love flying. Planes are my second home. It's like being in my bed. I can do my favorite activity—sleep. Except I hate waking up and my neck is half-broken and I look like a friggin' raptor from *Jurassic Park*. I have to have my Hello Kitty pillow because I take it everywhere, so now if I don't have it, I feel like the plane will crash. Plus it's comfy. And it's like traveling with a friend.

The thing I don't like about flying is if I get body-searched, and it's not a hot guy, I feel violated. But I get my entertainment watching people flip out at security.

I would like Virgin America to be my private airline, thank you. I officially love them. They play Usher while you check in. Party plane!

I feel like I could be a legit flight attendant. I'd look hot, and I'd make everyone buy $7 cocktails.

AIRPLANE MOMENTS

I was leaving Las Vegas with Ryder, and we were so upset to leave that we went to a bar and ripped shots, then we were loud and obnoxious the whole plane ride. When the plane landed some guy went, "Shut *up!*" And the whole plane started clapping. Kewl!

Trains

I don't take trains. They're weird. Like, how many asses sat on that seat?

Road Trips with Frankie

I'm always on the road for shows and appearances, so I got my Beema, Frankie, all decked out in zebra (he's so hot) and ready for cruisin'. I love my road trips. I get to listen to sick beats, open the windows and have the wind blowing when it's warm out, and have a good time with whoever's in the car. But I'll go crazy if I don't have good music so I make a few new CDs before every trip—one crazy electro/house-music CD; one love songs/trance/progressive house music; and one old-school, like 'N Sync and Backstreet Boys. I blast my beats and cuddle with my stuffed dog. My car has, legit, my entire closet in it.

My Beema, Frankie, rockin' zebra print.

Road trip! My slippers and my dad's bald head.

My driver thinks he's in NASCAR. I already shit myself three times.

10 THINGS I WON'T TRAVEL WITHOUT

Aussie, Paul Mitchell, or Salon Grafix shampoo and conditioner

Something animal print

Lots of chunky jewelry

Victoria's Secret lotion

Animal-print clothes

iPod or laptop

Hello Kitty pillow

Stuffed animals

Vibrator

Crocadilly, if it's a long trip so I can sleep with him between my legs

Omigod. The best thing ever is to sing at the top of your lungs to Dirty Dancing's "(I've Had) the Time of My Life."

MY FAVORITE PLACES

NEW YORK CITY. My all-time favorite place. My concrete jungle has the finest fist-pumpin' guidos!

L.A. The vibe is amazing. The people are hot. I love the nightlife, but I hate the traffic and fake people. Like I'm from New York, bitch, get real and tell me to fuck off instead of smiling to my face. All the trees look like broccoli.

VEGAS. I feel like a kid in a candy store there. It's edgy and everything goes, like me. The Palms Sky Villa is my home away from home. It has a friggin' pool in the room and club lights in the shower. It's an adult Chuck E. Cheese.

HAWAII. My eyelashes are floating somewhere in the Pacific right now. Hawaii is freakin' amazing. It's a place you go for a real getaway. The scenery is unreal, and you can see through the water.

SOUTH BEACH. The beach is sick and the night-life is one big party, like everyone's on spring break. And everyone's gorgeous and tan. They're nicer than Jersey people. New Jersey people are hard and rude. I missed my jerk-offs. And there are no guidos so I had to settle for lean cuisines.

My Hawaii look, LOL. Tryna do a hot pose with the concrete burning my ass. Kewl.

DISNEY WORLD. It makes me happy and I feel seven again!

THE JERSEY SHORE. The guido homeland! In Seaside, you have the hottest fist-pumping guido juiceheads in the world, the jerk-off attitude, the insane club scene with the best house music. And you have the boardwalk so you can shop and play like a little kid. But it's sleazy. That's why we call it Sleazeside.

Places I Don't Like

Places that are in the middle of nowhere. Like this little town in upstate Pennsylvania where I had a club appearance; I won't say the name, but it was like Hickville. There were like a hundred people at the club, and everyone was weird and pale and wore weird clothes.

Anywhere with a population of a thousand isn't a good scene. Friggin' crickets. They don't even have tanning salons.

One Place I'd Like to Go

Santiago, Chile, where I was born before being adopted by my Italian family.

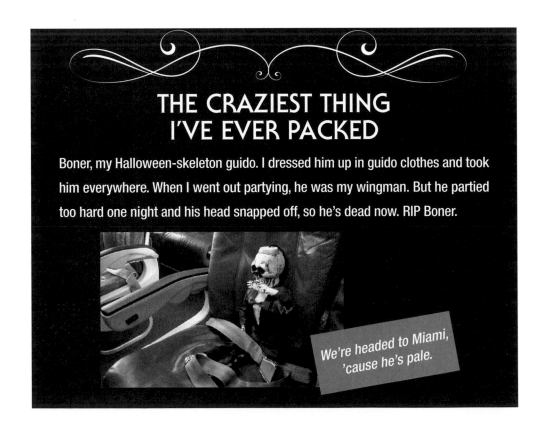

THE CRAZIEST THING I'VE EVER PACKED

Boner, my Halloween-skeleton guido. I dressed him up in guido clothes and took him everywhere. When I went out partying, he was my wingman. But he partied too hard one night and his head snapped off, so he's dead now. RIP Boner.

We're headed to Miami, 'cause he's pale.

Packing Like a Guidette

WHAT I TOOK ON MY VEGAS AND HAWAIIAN VACATION BEFORE FILMING SEASON 4

VEGAS:

Animal-print explosion!
Gaudy and sexy.
Animal-print
high boots and heels,
giant hoop earrings,
and bling!

HAWAII:

Sunglasses,
Hawaiian sundress,
bathing-suit cover-ups,
cute jewelry,
sexy wedges,
and a hat.

Captain Snooki

* I want to buy a yacht. Can you imagine me with my own yacht, like in the ocean, with a million guidos?

* Whaddup, bitches! Captain Snooki here. How do I fly this whore? Dance party!

If I owned an airport, I would Inspector Gadget the chairs and turn them into Tempur-Pedic beds.

6

My Life

IS A PARTY

* *Clubs, Parties, and Going Hollywood*

*A*ny day that ends in a *y* is a good day to party. *Party* ends in *y*. Like, "y" not?

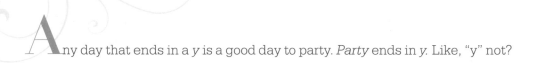

CLUBBING AND BARHOPPING
(Taking the Night with My Broads)

If you're a guidette, your life revolves around partying—going out on the week-ends, beating up the beat, hunting for guidos, going crazy with your girls.

When me and my girls go out, it's on like Donkey Kong. I've had the same friends forever and now Jenni, and we know how to party together, and we go haaaard. It's like get out of our way or, seriously, you're gonna get wounded by a fricken fist pump. My anthem is Pitbull's "Shut It Down" because I shut it down everywhere I go.

It doesn't come up "stripper pole" on my credit card, right? 'Cause my dad would be like "What the fuck?"

5 OF MY FAVORITE DIRTY, FILTHY DANCE BEATS

Flo Rida, "Turn Around"

Pitbull, "Shut It Down"

Deadmau5, Medina, "You and I"

Filo and Peri, "Anthem"

Jonas Steur, "Fall to Pieces" (my all-time favorite guidette track!!)

Amp It Up, Bitches! My Party Secrets

I KNOW THE BOUNCERS. The bouncers see me and they're like "The crazy girl's here!" The bouncers at Karma were letting us in when we were twenty. 'Cause they love when hot girls jump on them and hug them.

FROLICKING. We frolic everywhere—tree-branching, battling the beat, fist-pumping. We could be at the bar waiting for a drink and we're frolicking like friggin' lunatics, almost knocking people's eyeballs out.

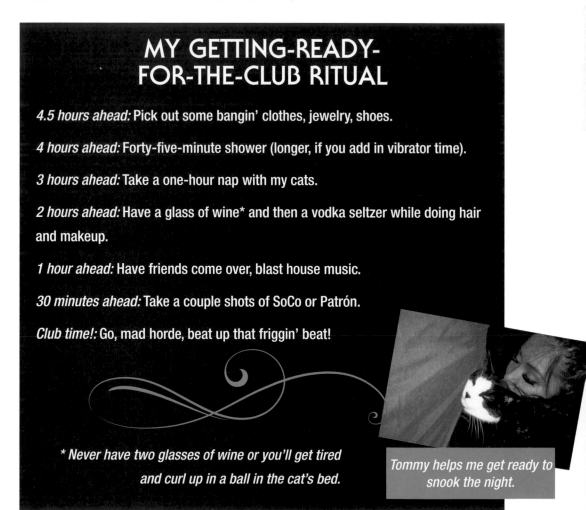

MY GETTING-READY-FOR-THE-CLUB RITUAL

4.5 hours ahead: Pick out some bangin' clothes, jewelry, shoes.

4 hours ahead: Forty-five-minute shower (longer, if you add in vibrator time).

3 hours ahead: Take a one-hour nap with my cats.

2 hours ahead: Have a glass of wine* and then a vodka seltzer while doing hair and makeup.

1 hour ahead: Have friends come over, blast house music.

30 minutes ahead: Take a couple shots of SoCo or Patrón.

Club time!: Go, mad horde, beat up that friggin' beat!

* Never have two glasses of wine or you'll get tired and curl up in a ball in the cat's bed.

Tommy helps me get ready to snook the night.

DANCING WITH GUYS. I don't dance with strange guys. It's creepy. I can't stand random guys humping your butt and getting a boner off your ass. I'd rather battle. If a guy comes over, my girls and I know each other's looks, like "He's okay" or "Omigod, creeper." I say I'm a lesbian if I don't want to hurt a guy's feelings. I use that a lot. Otherwise, I don't care. I'll say, "You're disgusting, get away from me."

I just realized. I fucking enjoy laughing.

MY FAVORITE PLACE TO HANG WITH MY GIRLS
Shadows on the Hudson. It has a New York City vibe in Poughkeepsie. It's classy and everybody's good-looking.

THE GUIDETTE WEEK

Every guidette knows the week starts on Thursday.

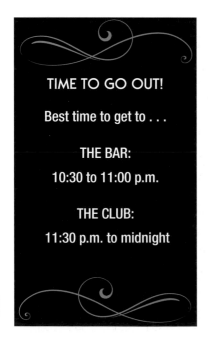

THURSDAY: Bar night with friends.

FRIDAY: House party *or* a movie night at home with friends.

SATURDAY: The Big Night! Go to clubs and go friggin' crazy and try not to get arrested.

SUNDAY: Options! Hangover/stay in and watch movies in bed all day *or* get up early and go shopping and hit the bar for Sunday Funday!

MON–WED: Tanning, gym, shopping, and saving money for Thursday through Sunday.

TIME TO GO OUT!

Best time to get to . . .

THE BAR:
10:30 to 11:00 p.m.

THE CLUB:
11:30 p.m. to midnight

PREGAMING IT. We've got our strategy down. We go to the club early and have drinks before everybody gets there, so when it's time to party, we're not fighting the hordes to get to the bar and waiting twenty minutes for drinks. I'm a Smurf, I could get stampeded. So we get to dance our asses off the whole time. Sometimes we *pre*-pre-game—we have drinks and start the party before we leave the house—except the person who's driving, usually me.

A HOLD-YOUR-HEELS NIGHT. If either me or Ryder says, "Hold my heels," that means it's *on*, like one of us is in the mood to friggin' destroy the place. And then it's like a contagious disease. She'll hold my heels while I go crazy, and then I'll hold her heels, and everybody parts like the Red Sea. And you know shit's gonna go down; we'll dance on tables, anything can happen. The backflips might be coming out. (If you're too buzzed to remember you're wearing granny panties? Kewl.)

*I look over and I see like
hair being pulled
and all this shit, and I'm like
"Oh my god, how do I get in?!"*

MY OTHER PARTY SECRETS

✳ Be the one to start the party—crank up the music, start dancing, start a game.

✳ Be open to trying new things.

✳ Even if you're shy, walk in a room like you own it. But not like a bitch.

✳ Don't just stay with your group. Mingle with everyone and make friends.

✳ Diva status, bitches!

My Favorite Places to Eat, Drink, Play, and Shop

SUSHISAMBA, New York. I go there all the time, it's my all-time favorite restaurant. Best drinks ever. You can order a whole cocktail rack and sample every drink.

WET REPUBLIC at MGM Grand, Las Vegas. Everyone's ready to drink and dance any time of day. It's kind of like a Jersey scene.

CLUBS IN NEW YORK CITY. The best clubs are 1 Oak, Tenjune, Butter, and Pacha, where all the guidos go.

OCEAN'S TEN, Miami Beach. Hot, sexy crowd, and the friggin' awesomest drink I ever had—the Bulldog. A big-ass margarita with two upside-down Coronas. Legit, I drank it and I was upside down.

WOODBURY COMMON in Central Valley, New York, for shopping. I lived in Juicy, Bebe, and Armani. Except I can't go to malls anymore, people are crazy.

DAVE & BUSTERS, anywhere. It's an arcade for adults. You get drunk and play skee ball and try to win stuff. Crocadilly was born there.

KATSUYA, L.A. It's classy and has great food and drinks and a great vibe. There's always celebrities there.

NOVE ITALIANO at the Palms, Las Vegas. It's very Italian, they have the best ravioli and gravy on the planet. Great view of Vegas. And leopard-print chairs. Friggin' no-brainer.

MOON in Las Vegas. Vegas clubs are insane. The party never stops, you can go club-hopping at 10 a.m.

CARLO'S BAKESHOP in Hoboken, New Jersey. The cannolis are sick. Creamy and sweet and beyond amazing. I want them right now.

GOING HOLLYWOOD

Clubs

Nightlife in L.A. and Vegas is insane, like dance on tables in your underwear. They play the best music, the vibe is wild, anything goes, you always see celebrities. I think I've partied with pretty much everyone in Hollywood.

GUARD YOUR BOOBS, BITCHES!

This is how I shake hands with people. (Hey, I'm a shrimp, and your boobs are in my face!)

Parties

Hollywood parties are all the same, they're not like parties with your friends. It's so fake. It's all celebrities, you can't mingle, and everyone wants a picture.

I was so excited to go to the Deadmau5 party after the VMAs because I'm in love with Deadmau5, but I was so nervous to meet him, no words came out. Pauly had to talk for me. I felt like a friggin' idiot!

MY FAVORITE PARTY OF THE YEAR. My birthday party at Pacha, in the VIP room! My dad got a party bus and we went around picking everybody up and had cocktails all the way to New York City. (We pregamed it!) Sean Kingston sang (LOVE him!), I got to dance and party with like a hundred of my family and friends, then we had an after-party in the hotel rooms all night. I still didn't recover. I had the most amazing cake that Buddy from *Cake Boss* did. It had my head on top with a poof on it. I was like "Nobody eat my head."

My Favorite Celebrities to Hang Out With

My *Jersey Shore* roomies definitely. We know how to party from living together, and we go crazy. We're like fist-pumping machines. And we're all tan. And hot. And I got to be really close with Kat DeLuna this year. She's awesome and gorgeous *and* tan.

My Favorite Events of the Past Year

NUMBER ONE BY FAR: WRESTLEMANIA. The vibe the crowd gives you is insane. I got to meet John Cena and the Rock. Gorilla freakin' central! Hello—Snooki sandwich! I'm not even kidding.

THE CMAS. *The* most fun award show I've ever been to. I'm a closet country-music fan. *Love* Carrie Underwood, Taylor Swift, Josh Turner. And I got to meet Tim McGraw! Country music *ape*.

THE GRAMMYS. Sway is a gorilla juicehead. The dressing-up-all-glamorous part isn't really me. But I got to meet my and Jenni's crush, David Guetta. Nicki Minaj grabbed my boobs (love her!). And Lady Gaga waved at us from her egg. That was insane!

Waiter goes "Lemon or lime?"
Me: "What's the green one?"

Honestly, like who hides in a bush? Only me. I will pee in a bush, I will poop in a bush, and I will hide in a bush. I do fucked-up shit. I don't even know what's wrong with me.

NEW YEAR'S EVE 2011. MTV asked me to be in the ball, but I didn't want to look like a hamster. I totally looked like a friggin' hamster. And the crowd was right under me, so I felt like they could see up my kooka. But I didn't die in the ball, so it was a good night.

I'll be in a store and hear one beat of a Deadmau5 or Kaskade track and freeze like I just heard a mating call.

My Signature Drink

The Pickletini
(my own creation)

TWO WARNINGS:

No lightweights allowed,

and you better like pickles!

✳ 1 part vodka
✳ ½ part pickle juice
   from a jar of pickles

Cheers
(and pickle puckers)!

7

Snookin'
FOR LOVE

* *Guido Juiceheads and Gorillas*

'm addicted to guys. Even though they can be a huge friggin' pain in the ass. But once I see sexy, sweaty gorillas, I forget all about it. I'm a sucka for a guy with a guinea T, muscles, and a backward hat. Or if he's legit, fresh to death. Obviously he has to be tan. I'll make an exception for Adam Sandler. He's pale, and he's not a guido, but I'd smush that.

I'm thinking of turning lesbian. I swear.

Mario's my #1 Mexican guido.

It's kind of like a disease to snook for love. It's worse than a staph infection.

MY RULES ON SNOOKIN' FOR LOVE

Know Your Species

Guido juiceheads and gorilla juiceheads are two different creatures. A guido is into his tan, his hair, his style, and dancing to house music. A gorilla is more into the gym, tanning, his muscles, and himself. Gorillas would smush with themselves if they could.

I go out with guidos. Pauly's a guido. Ronnie's a gorilla.

Then you have the apes. Fist pumps for gorillas over thirty. I told Regis Philbin he was a hot ape. LMAO!

Where are the juiceheads? I don't see any fucking guido juiceheads. You woke me up for nothing.

Those guys that are too big and musclely, that's a walrus. It's like, bro, if you can't put your two hands behind your back and touch them, you're no gorilla, you're a fricken walrus. Slow your roll.

Is He a Man or a Friggin' Toddler?

Seriously. There's men and then there's boys, which is most of the guys I've ever gone out with. Boys suck the life out of you because, legit, they're still friggin' nursing, and guess what? You're the fricken boob. Boys are insecure and jealous and all about themselves, and they want to stay twelve forever. Men make you laugh, boys make you cry. Men make you feel alive and protect you and have your back and are confident enough to let you do *you*. And they smush better. Just sayin'.

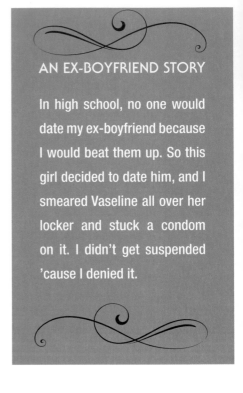

AN EX-BOYFRIEND STORY

In high school, no one would date my ex-boyfriend because I would beat them up. So this girl decided to date him, and I smeared Vaseline all over her locker and stuck a condom on it. I didn't get suspended 'cause I denied it.

Flirt Like a Bitch

I used to be really forward and go right up to guys. Then me and Ryder figured out that if you're nice to guys, they get bored. If you're a bitch, they try to impress you. If you're like 'Ew, get away, fuck you,' then they chase you. It really works.

I have a love-hate relationship with jerk-offs.

How to Get Other Guidettes' Paws off Your Guido

Omigod. If I'm at a club and I see girls tryin' to talk to my guy, I get in front of their faces like I'm gonna knock them out. I saw my boyfriend talking to a bunch of girls and I ran over and said, "I'm Nicole, I'm the girlfriend, can I help you?" like a total bitch. And they walked away. And my boyfriend was like "You idiot, those were my best friends from high school."

Guys are dicks.
No wonder the lesbian rate
is so high in this country.

Gorilla Central
WHERE THE GUIDOS ARE

1. Seaside Heights, New Jersey

2. Belmar, New Jersey

3. Brooklyn, New Yawk

4. Bronx, New Yawk

5. Any North Jersey beach in the summer

6. Long Island

DTS: My Pass/Fail Checklist

(IF I'M "SINGLE NICOLE," NOT "COMMITTED NICOLE")

FAIL.
LIKE DTS AIN'T
HAPPENIN', JERK-OFF.

* From afar he's a ho, up close he's a no.
* He grabs my ass (if you're not my boyfriend, Corona in the eyeballs!).
* He's hairy (I don't want to cuddle and hair goes up my nose).
* He calls me Snooki (if he does it in bed, he better hide his balls).
* He doesn't dance with you, he just sits there. Crickets!
* He smells like BO. Take a fucking shower!
* He goes off and talks to other girls in the club and then comes back (get lost, asshole).
* Talking to him is like talking to a box of rocks.
* When you kiss, he sticks his tongue down your throat and makes you want to throw up. Good-bye.

Not baby-daddy material (still love you, bitch!).

* He's hot. *Rawr!*
* He makes me laugh.
* He pays for drinks (real guidos don't let girls pay).
* He stays with you the whole night (and ditches his friends for you).
* He's dressed fresh to death. Like totally pimpin'. Faded-out jeans, kinda ripped, nice shoes, an Ed Hardy–style T with sparkles/rhinestones, a gold cross, and spiky hair, like "I rock shit."
* He's a good spooner, and a good kisser!

PASS.
DTS!

I want my relationship to be just like Titanic, Avatar, *and* Just Married.

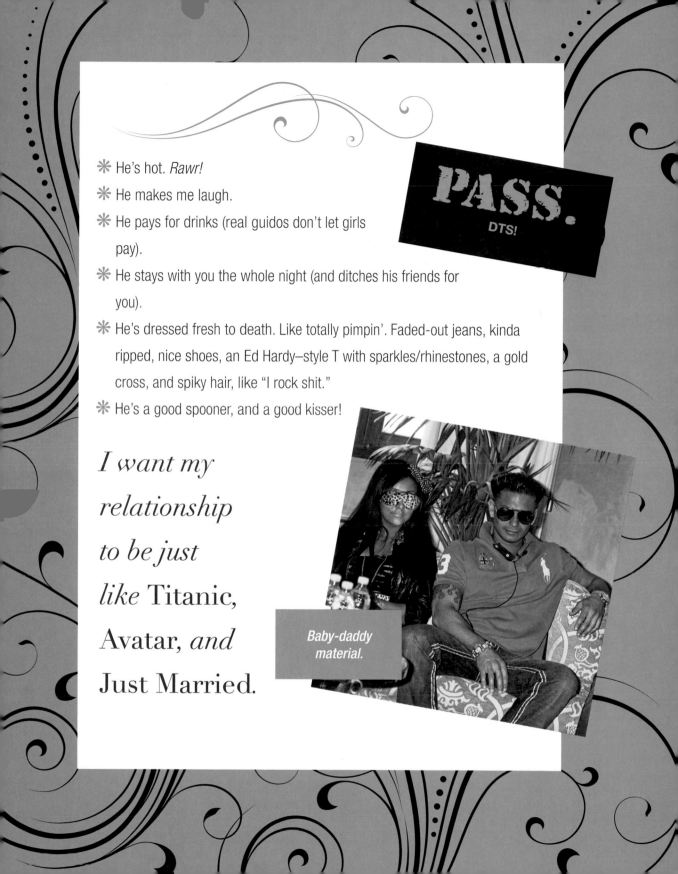

Baby-daddy material.

My Most Important Qualities in a Guy (Not Like Crickets, the Real Deal)

LOOKS. Let's be honest, I don't want to date a scary person. I want a short, guido juicehead.

I DON'T BELIEVE OPPOSITES ATTRACT. Do you really think I'd date a pale person that doesn't like Ed Hardy? That would be awkward.

HE HAS TO BE TAN. Tan, orange, whatever. I want tan babies.

HE CAN'T BE BORING. My personality is so big and so friggin' out there, he has to be dorky and silly and like to laugh.

HE HAS TO HAVE SOME EDUCATION AND BE SMART.

If you don't want to cuddle,
thanks for the braciola,
but no dinner dates
with you and me . . .
good-bye . . . never see you again.

HE'S MY BEST FRIEND AND I CAN TELL HIM ANYTHING.

HE FIST-PUMPS AND IS A GOOD DANCER. (Not like Mike, like he's poking some Amazon broad in the boobs. I mean actually dance.)

It's like fitting a watermelon in a pinhole.

HE LOVES HIS MOTHER. That's a good sign. And he's close with his family. And he likes mine.

HE'LL LEGIT FROLIC.

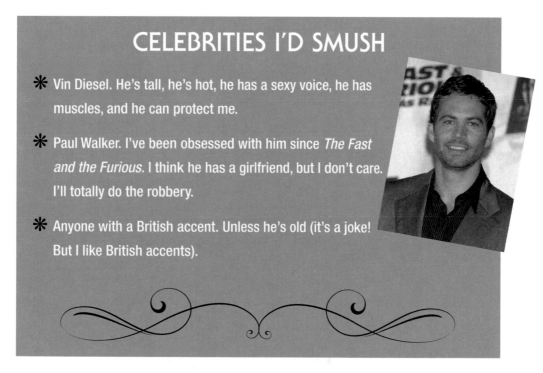

CELEBRITIES I'D SMUSH

✻ Vin Diesel. He's tall, he's hot, he has a sexy voice, he has muscles, and he can protect me.

✻ Paul Walker. I've been obsessed with him since *The Fast and the Furious*. I think he has a girlfriend, but I don't care. I'll totally do the robbery.

✻ Anyone with a British accent. Unless he's old (it's a joke! But I like British accents).

Whoever I have babies with has to be Italian. I want my kids' last name to have a vowel in it. And be tanned obviously.

HE PROTECTS ME.

HE'S SEXY AND JUICY AND ROMANTIC.

HE LIKES TO SLEEP IN AND WATCH MOVIES IN BED.

HE'S A NICE JERK-OFF. He has to have *some* jerk-off in him. I'm a friggin' guidette from New York.

HIS LAST NAME ENDS IN A VOWEL.

My man ♥.

Bitches, Boys, and Bullies
MY 3 WORST HIGH SCHOOL MOMENTS

✳ In ninth grade, the older girls hated me because I was popular. So they started a nasty rumor about me and a senior boy and started calling me Stinkin' Incan and wrote "Nicole's a slut" on the walls. I was like "I never even had sex." They made my freshman year a living hell. That's why I hate freakin' bullies. But it made me a stronger person. Thank you, bitches!

✳ I went to another school's prom, and the boy's mother helped me get ready upstairs, and I felt like a princess, like he watched me walk down the stairs, and it was so romantic like in the movies. And then I tripped down the steps and my legs went up in the air, and I had white granny panties on, and I started crying. But who the frig wears granny panties to the prom, they look like friggin' diapers. He never talked to me again after the prom. It was probably the granny panties.

✳ My first time having sex was in eleventh grade at prom with this boy I really liked. And of course, like an idiot, I thought he'd be madly in love with me afterward. I mean, hello, your first time. But then next time I saw him in class, he ignored me. I was like kewl, life sucks, boys are douche bags. I definitely regret it.

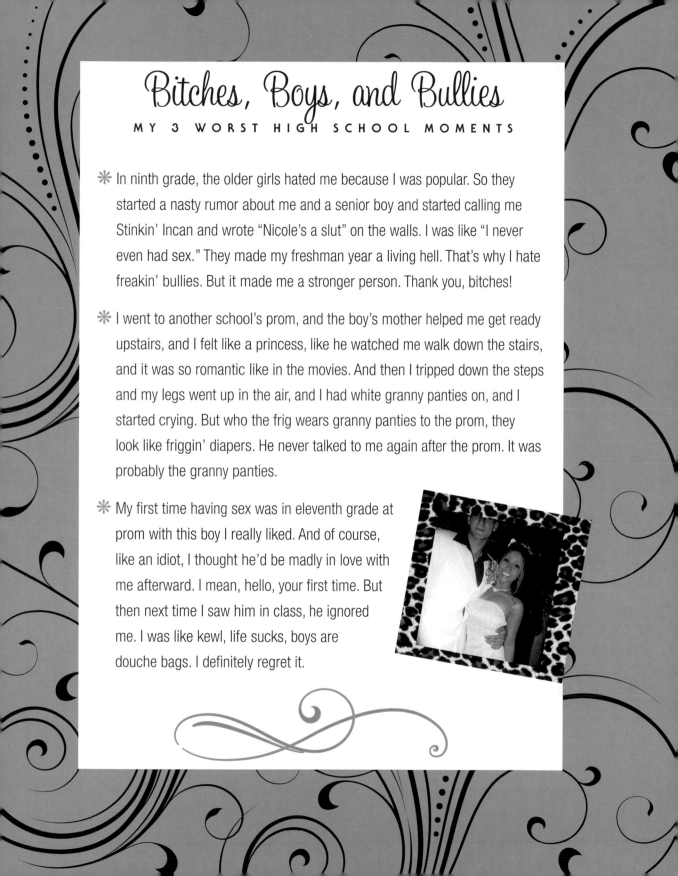

MY BANGIN' RECIPES

People think I can't cook, but I get a bad rap. I can cook a few things, but I need a recipe. If you give me the step-by-step, I got it covered. I'll cook Thanksgiving if you give me a play-by-play about what the frig I have to do. Just don't yell at me if you get poisoned. It's the thought that counts.

I know how to make only two things without a recipe, but I perfected them. You can try to make them as bangin' as mine, but I doubt it.

My Bangin' Grilled Cheese

* **TONS OF BUTTER**
* **BREAD**
* **CHEESE**

Butter up the pan. Then butter the bread, both pieces, and slap 'em in there. You want to make sure they're nice and crispy. Then you put the cheese on top of one. When it melts a little, put the other piece of bread on top, and flip it till it looks legit.

(This is a good meal for when you come home from the club at 5:00 a.m.!)

My Bangin' Chicken Cutlets

* **3 EGGS**
* **GRATED PARMESAN CHEESE**
* **BREAD CRUMBS WITH ITALIAN SEASONING**
* **4 CHICKEN CUTLETS**
* **CANOLA OR OLIVE OIL**

Put three eggs in a bowl, and after you mix them, sprinkle in grated Parmesan cheese. Put the bread crumbs in another bowl and sprinkle in some Parmesan cheese (I love grated cheese). Then do like a wax-on, wax-off. Dip the chicken in the eggs, then in the bread crumbs, then slap it in the pan. Next one, dip the chicken in the eggs, then the bread crumbs, then slap it in the pan. The pan should already have oil in it and be warmed up. Then you just fry those suckers until they're nice and crispy! Nomnomnomnom!

8

GTL
According to Me

* **GYM:** Smushing (the best exercise)

TAN: Yes

~~**LAUNDRY**~~: Could I get a mimosa, please?

From watching the show, you wouldn't know it because I act like a princess (um, I am a princess), but I'm also a sports freak and a tomboy. I grew up riding ATVs, snow-mobiles, being athletic, and watching the Amazin's—the New York Mets. I like to play and get dirty, and I'll try any sport. I love the gym, and I kill it in step classes and Zumba.

Getting My Ass Kicked

For the first three seasons, I didn't GTL at all when we were filming the show. I figured we're drinking ourselves to death anyway. And I'd rather fricken sleep. When filming's over, I

MY WORKOUT ROUTINE

* One-half hour on the treadmill.

* One-half hour on the elliptical.

* Then I hit the strength train-ing—legs, squats, ass, arms. (There are these ab exercises where you lift your legs up high and tighten your abs—omigod, almost as good as a vibrator.)

* Then crunches (like a thousand of them!).

* If I'm not feeling the gym, I have a full-on one-hour dance party in my room. I crank up the house music and pretend I'm onstage in the club and every-body's watchin'!

look at myself and I'm like "Omigod, I'm round." I get in serious detox mode. I cut down on alcohol and I'm like obsessed with working out. I have to have a trainer because if I don't, I'm watching hot gorillas bend over the whole time. Honestly? Who can friggin' work out with sweaty juiceheads all over the place flexing their muscles and distracting me? It's like you died and went to guido heaven.

People don't get it about tiny girls. If I were stretched out, I'd look like a supermodel. But I'm compact.

I have to work out with my iPod. Some days I work out to house music because it reminds me of the shore and bikinis. But Foo Fighters or Goo Goo Dolls are better because they get me pumped up and ready to kick someone's ass. I think I'm Rocky. When I was lifting weights, my trainer told me to breathe deep and I accidentally spit in his face. He said people farted on him, but nobody ever spit in his face. Kewl.

When you work out, don't be prissy because you just look like an idiot. Unless your crush is there. Then make sure you wear your false eyelashes.

I go to the gym every day because if I don't, I feel like I'm gross. But not the weekend because I might be hungover (or I might be shopping). Because, let's be honest, you need some balance! If you work hard, you can play hard.

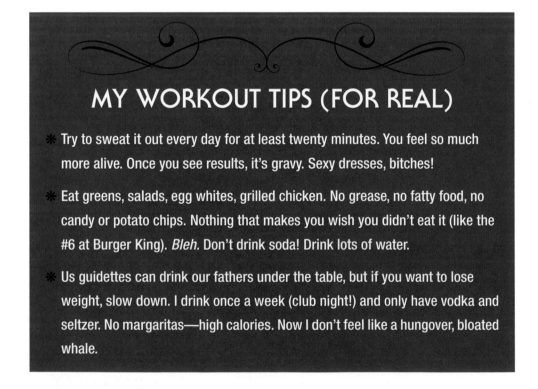

MY WORKOUT TIPS (FOR REAL)

✳ Try to sweat it out every day for at least twenty minutes. You feel so much more alive. Once you see results, it's gravy. Sexy dresses, bitches!

✳ Eat greens, salads, egg whites, grilled chicken. No grease, no fatty food, no candy or potato chips. Nothing that makes you wish you didn't eat it (like the #6 at Burger King). *Bleh.* Don't drink soda! Drink lots of water.

✳ Us guidettes can drink our fathers under the table, but if you want to lose weight, slow down. I drink once a week (club night!) and only have vodka and seltzer. No margaritas—high calories. Now I don't feel like a hungover, bloated whale.

HOW TO BE A
TOMBOY GUIDETTE

I love playing and watching sports. First of all, there are hot guys running around in tight pants. Yum! If you get bored with the sport, you can just check out their asses. It's like friggin' porn. Football players are gorillas and they know how to kick shit. Baseball players know how to hit home runs, and wrestlers get down on the floor, take control, and get the biznaz done! (Like Jionni, yum!).

I was born a Mets fan. My grandfather was a die-hard Mets fan, and I wasn't even ten or eleven when I'd go to his house and he'd be like "You're my girl, and we're gonna cheer our Mets on." I'll rep my Amazin's till the day I die. My fantasy is to be in a room full of Mets players from the last fifteen years. By myself.

My poppy, my cousin, and me; probably cheering on our Mets!

I look like a hot, drunk baseball player right now, and I'm lovin' it. *Batter up, bitches!*

MY FAVORITE SNACKS
WHEN I'M WORKING OUT

Rice cakes with peanut butter

Celery and dip

Broccoli with ranch dressing

Have a Crush on a Sports Guido

I'm obsessed with Robin Ventura, who played for the Mets when I was a freshman in high school. He's not your typical guido, and he's older, but if I got him for one day, he'd be in friggin' mint condition! My sports guido crush is John Cena, the wrestler (what up bro, love u!). He's got the tan (sometimes) and the muscles—he's a friggin' hot gorilla.

Do a Sport

Guidettes that do sports are sexy and badass. Sports give you strength, endurance, and flexibility. Hello! DTS (or attacking a bitch like a squirrel monkey).

My Favorite Sports

CHEERLEADING WAS MY LIFE. I competed in gymnastics for eight years in school, then started cheerleading and became captain of my cheer squad. I'm obsessed with cheerleading—I loved being a flier, I love tumbling, I love cheers, I love making faces. I was a strict captain; I was like Kirsten Dunst in *Bring It On.* I got pissed if the girls did the cheers wrong, I wanted us to win trophies. Instead of doing homework, I'd be home making up cheers and dances.

My last home football game as a senior. Wah!

> *I'm not normally a bitch, but if you're following me in the gym with your old man hard-ons and cameras, I will kick you in your shins. That is all.*

SNOWBOARDING AND SLEDDING. I love winter sports and I love snow! When you snowboard, it's tomboy status. You fall, you act cute in front of the guys, and then when's it's time to ride, get out of my way, whore! It's on.

WRESTLEMANIA. It's seriously my next calling. I used to watch WrestleMania when Dave Batista was on—the man was a gorilla, tattoos down both arms, like mad hot; he's old now, but he's probably still hot! So when they asked me to do it, I started watching it, and it was pretty sick. I thought "No way can I do those moves!" But I love doing shit people don't expect me to do. Then I got in the ring and was like "I get to kick someone's ass and not get arrested? I was fricken made for this!" First of all, it's gorilla fucking central; even the women wrestlers are hot. And the outfits are *sick*! Rhinestones, sexy, *and* animal print? And then I've got my Jersey attitude, my gymnastics, and my cheerleading skills, and JWoww taught me some sick moves, so I got in the ring and I friggin' brought it. I hadn't done backflips in like six years and just whipped it out like nothing. It was insane.

GETTING SPANXED

We did a basketball game one day, and I wanted to impress the boys, so instead of wearing the Spanx like everyone else, I wore hot-pink underwear and did my back handsprings, and everyone gasped, like they saw my vagina. I was like "Cool." And then I got yelled at by my coach and had to go put Spanx on.

Dress Cute

You can totally guidette-it-up in sports gear. For baseball, you wear cute short-shorts, a cute top, a bangin' cap, and you gotta rock the knee-high socks!! Sexy! For football, same thing, but I put my hair up in a hot, sexy sloppy bun and smear black under my eyes like a football player. It means "I'm ready to win, bitch." And I'll tackle your ass. Just like in the club if you go near my man.

My School Sports Moments

✴ I killed it in middle-school dodgeball. I dodged it by doing backflips.

✴ I loved powder-puff, where the girls play football and the boys cheer. When I have knee pads on, something's going down. It was the junior girls' chance to kick the senior girls' asses and kill each other on the field, legit.

✴ There was no better way to shut up those bitches from rival squads than with a better routine, cheer, and stunts. My girls would do twenty touches in a row while I did back handsprings up and down on the basketball court until I couldn't walk. They called me Dizzy Polizzi.

9

Outside
THE SPOTLIGHT

* *AKA Chill Time!*

Shocker alert! I'm not really a party girl.

Okay . . . I have my days when I want to tear it up and go batshit fucking crazy. I mean I'll try anything once. But honestly? I'm really a homebody. I'm like a split personality. Sometimes I feel like partying, but the rest of the time I'm a normal girl. I like to chill and be quiet and stay home and watch movies in bed, or be a dork with my family and friends, or spoon with my cats.

Even when I'm on the road doing events, I need my space. I'll curl up into a friggin' ball in a garbage can just to be quiet. I'll hide anywhere. If I can get in my Hello Kitty pajamas and watch movies and look at pictures of my cats and take a nap and recharge, then it's on, and I'm ready to hang again. I need my naps, 'cause having a good time is my priority wherever I am. Like seriously? Why isn't everybody having more fun? I don't care if you're twenty or ninety, live it up. I hate when people are so stuffy and serious, like they're too classy to have fun. Get real. Take the friggin' stick out of your butt hole. Laugh a little. You're gonna be extinct one day.

I'm way too excited for life right now.

I travel so much that I'm rarely home anymore, so I really miss my family and my cats and my friends and my bed. I'll come home and see my furniture and be so happy that I want to make out with it. I'm weird. I know.

My Parents

My parents are my absolute best friends. They adopted me when I was six months old, and they always let me be me. That's why I think I'm so strong and confident, because they didn't try to mold me into something else. Unless you count growing up in an Italian house and turning into a meatball, even though I'm Chilean! Guido is in my blood.

I LOVE ANIMALS!

I seriously *love* animals. I'd rather chill with animals than people. They're so innocent, and they love you unconditionally. I was working as a vet tech assistant and I had a year left of vet tech school at community college when *Jersey Shore* started. I loved operating on sick animals and making them better and delivering babies. I wanted to take all the animals home with me. Someday I'd like to finish school, but I'd like to open up my own hospital and help as many animals as I can.

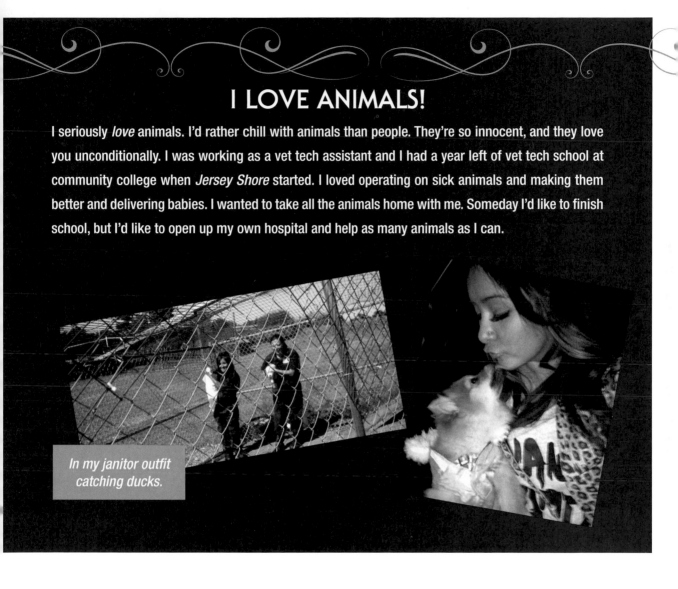

In my janitor outfit catching ducks.

Omigod. The lightning isn't normal right now. Aliens.

My mom, Helen. I gave her a poof for the club. Cougar status!

My mom and me, age eighteen, at my last home football game.

MAMA SNOOKS. My mom, Helen, is definitely one of my best friends. Even though we're different and she sometimes doesn't agree, she just gets me. She's conservative. I get my heart from her. It's hard for us to be mean or stay mad at people, and we're both klutzes and we're both always losing shit. One time me and my mom went on a photo shoot and we were trying all these poses, and she fell and flipped on her ass, so we were like "Kewl," and we did the shoot on the floor. I try to have her go out on dates. She's been single since I was thirteen. Sometimes I'm like "Mom, you need to have sex."

PAPA SNOOKS. I'm a total daddy's girl. My dad, Andy, is a retired guido. He's like boss status. He's where I get all my personality from—he's outgoing, he's a big flirt, and he likes to have a good time. I'm definitely my dad's child. We get into horrible fights because we're too alike, we're hardheads, but then we make up like nothing happened. When we go on the road together, we have a good time. I buy him guido clothes and dress him up. He's a firefighter, so I get to hang out at the firehouse with the firemen gorillas.

Two guidos in Vegas.

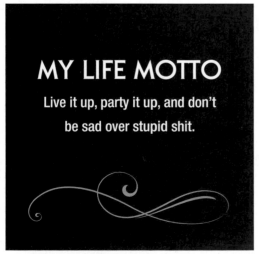

MY LIFE MOTTO

Live it up, party it up, and don't be sad over stupid shit.

Guidette-in-Training

Growing up, I was really shy and quiet (I was so shy, I was terrified of going to the doctor). I did well in school, I had lots of friends, I went to church. I was even an altar girl. Who would've thought I'd become the party girl of America? Except that I had a guido for a dad. And I was really cute. And I was tan, so anything's possible.

Armstrong
CEILING TILE
Armstrong
CEILING TILE
Armstrong
CEILING TILE

I still love playing
in boxes.

My Broads

My girls keep me sane. I don't care how busy I get, girl time will always be priority. It's my favorite time. I've had the same best friends forever—Ryder, Stephanie, Danielle, Amy, Franki, Kiersten, Katie, Kristin (who I met a few years ago in Jersey), and now Jenni. I couldn't survive without them. Once you get famous, it's hard to make friends because you don't know who's being real, so me and my friends have always been there for each other no matter what shit goes down, with boys, life, whatever. That's why I'll always be close with my roomies from the show, because we're going through the same stuff with fame and the paparazzi. Jenni's like my big sister, because she's older and she's been through everything I go through, so she gives great advice.

And my girls know how to have fun. We are balls-to-the-walls insane. Me and Jenni yell in each other's face and laugh hysterically (and pee behind bar counters). Me and Ryder are total weirdos—we'll frolic anywhere, and we have our own weird language. *Meh!* All my girlfriends are like family.

Hangin' with My girls; Our Favorite Activities

Listen to music, take over bars, act crazy, and take pictures, and everyone else thinks we're obnoxious.

Watch movies in the basement with popcorn, no makeup, being lazy.

Dear JWoww, Do your boobs miss me? 'Cause the pillows on my bed aren't the same. Love, Nicole.

Get our nails done and talk about boys and make fun of how stupid they are.

Have drinks at Chili's.

Go to a bar in the middle of the week and take over the jukebox and go crazy, and people storm out, so it becomes our bar.

Sit by the pool, barbecue, and invite friends over and play beer pong.

My Four-Legged Guidos

My cats are my world. They're my three mobsters, they're always there for me. When I'm home, we hang out. I got Rocky when I was ten. I got Tommy and Vito as a birthday present when I was nineteen; they're brothers, and they look like they're wearing tuxedos.

Rocky. Me and Rocky grew up together. I would die without him. He's my best friend. He doesn't mind if I have a boyfriend, we have an open relationship. But I hate when he watches me hook up. He stares at me. Or if it's vibrator time, he'll just stare at me, and I'm like "Rocky, get out." Rocky's the only one who gets dressed up. He has a leopard-print hoodie because he's #1. You have to dress Rocky up. He's fresh to death, and his tail looks like a raccoon's. He's husband material.

Vito. Vito's the bitch, he's my gay best friend. I think he's gay, he's always licking Rocky's butt hole. And he's scared of everything. He's really prissy.

Tommy. Tommy reminds me of an old drunk man because he's crazy and he's horny all the time, but he's the best cuddler. Someone on Twitter said he was ugly and I blocked them. Don't talk shit about my cat; I'll go squirrel monkey on your ass.

Vito lounging on my zebra print, like a good gay best friend.

My mobsters. Vito left, Tommy right, Rocky in front.

Molesting my husband Rocky. He's so hot.

Don't wear the hood, bro. You look like a peasant woman.

Tommy looks horny and drunk.

Rocky pretending he's on the runway in his leopard hoodie.

Mommy's Little Bitch— the Youngest of My Babies

9 FACTS ABOUT GIA

1. She's a Teacup Pomeranian. She's boss-lady princess bitch.

2. She's not allowed on my bed because she pees.

3. She used to get all the clothes, but she hates to wear clothes so I stopped buying them. She likes to be naked because she's a slut.

4. If she doesn't get her way, she'll bark and bite, and she needs attention at all times. She's like her mommy.

5. When I got her, she was so tiny and so innocent. Now she needs a little chat with Cesar the dog whisperer.

6. She poses when I take pictures of her.

7. She knows what's up. She goes after the big gorilla doggies, and she's always trying to smush with Mr. Zebra.

8. She growls in her sleep. I think she has nightmares about the bitches in the dog park who stole her teddy bear.

9. She's a legit guidette. She attacked a horse.

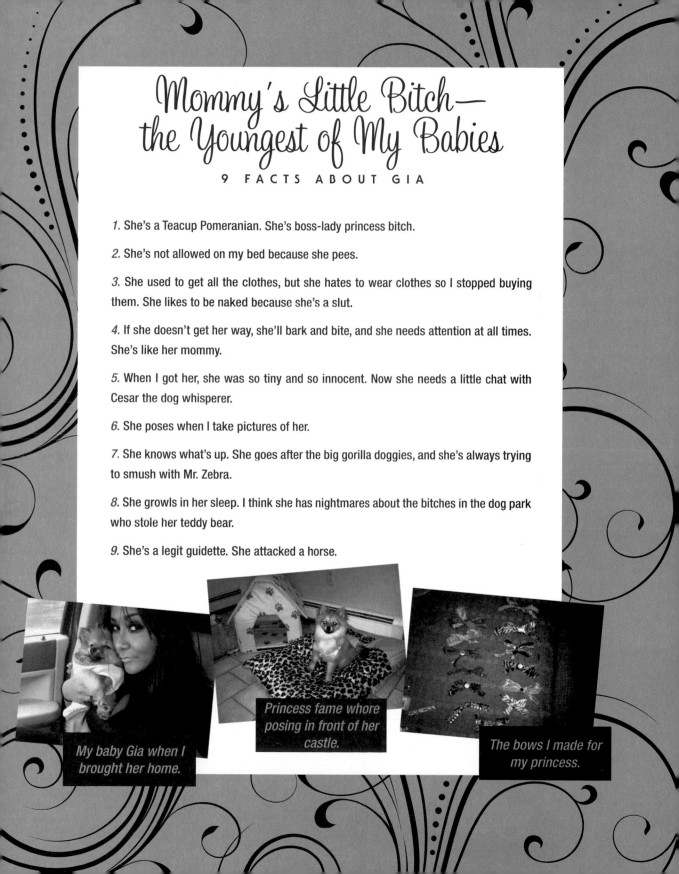

My baby Gia when I brought her home.

Princess fame whore posing in front of her castle.

The bows I made for my princess.

How I Met Ryder

Ryder hated me when I first met her! Her boyfriend (who was my friend) had an extra ticket to Deadmau5, and he invited me 'cause I'm friggin' obsessed with Deadmau5. And I got there and Ryder gave me dirty looks the entire time. I kept trying to be nice to her; I was like "What's *wrong* with her?" She thought I hooked up with her boyfriend, which I didn't. (If you're hot, girls always think you hooked up with their boyfriend. So fricken annoying.) After a few drinks, she warmed up to me, we made out, and we've been tearin' it up since. We're both insane.

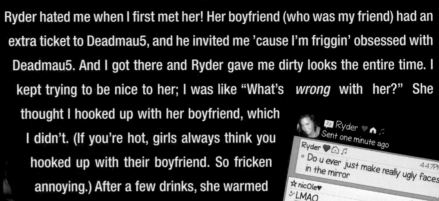

Our cricket face.

This is why we're best friends.

What if I just randomly opened my window and screamed, "It's my money and I need it now!"

MY LIFE GOALS

People think I'm just lucky, like stuff falls in my lap, but honestly? I'm a hard worker, and I've always had goals (besides boys and fried pickles). You know how they say if you reach for the stars, you'll land on the moon? Well, I'm landin' my ass on the freakin' sun. At least I'll get tan.

This is my list right now.

✳ *Get married by twenty-six or twenty-seven.* Get pregnant right away, have four or five guido/guidette babies, live in a nice house, and hopefully film it. If my babies don't come out tan, I'll spray them.

✳ *Be a MILF.* That's not a joke, I really want to be a MILF.

✳ *Open a cheerleading gym.* Or start my own cheerleading association and have competitions for all-star cheerleading. That's a passion that will never die. And it comes in handy in life; it teaches you how to do back handsprings to get past bouncers.

✳ *Build an empire.* I want to have a line of hair, skin-care, and tanning products, and of clothing. So *everyone* can look hot and there will be no

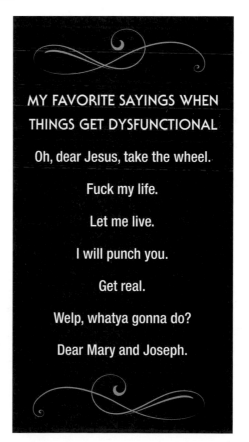

MY FAVORITE SAYINGS WHEN THINGS GET DYSFUNCTIONAL

Oh, dear Jesus, take the wheel.

Fuck my life.

Let me live.

I will punch you.

Get real.

Welp, whatya gonna do?

Dear Mary and Joseph.

more wars. But also, because I can't get a normal job after this. Could you see me sitting behind a desk? (Only if it's the fricken White House!)

✳ *Have my own animal hospital.* So I can help lots of animals and animal babies.

✳ *Do spin-off shows.* Me and Jenni got a spinoff that comes out in 2012. I always wanted my own show, and now I get to have a show with my boo! We wanted to get a place together anyway, so the show will follow us living together and just being ourselves when we're not at the shore. It will be dysfunctional and it will be freakin' amazing! And I also want future spinoffs of my future guidette babies.

✳ *Act in comedies.* I'm a really good actor and I'm funny, and I want to act in something I can be appreciated for. I want a Will Ferrell career, like doing funny movies, but improv, not scripted. Or a sitcom like *The Office.* I don't want to remember lines.

✳ *Have an animated character in a movie.* Like if I were a *Finding Nemo* character, I'd totally rock it. Hollywood could use a guidette fish.

✳ *Be boss lady of the world!*

I never expected this amazing ride to last this long (and fuck you, haters, who talked shit!). I don't take anything for granted and I'm beyond grateful every day. I have lots of stories to tell my grandkids (I'll still be rockin' my animal print, my poof, my six-inch heels, and a tan. Just sayin'). But I'm gonna keep tryin' to take over the world and do things people don't expect me to do. Why not? If I succeed, great. If I don't, kewl. I can say I tried it.

I learned a lot, and I think I'm becoming a better person. Like when I started *Jersey Shore*, I was twenty-one and homesick and terrified to be on my own. But I was forced to grow up, and every season I feel I've matured a lot.

But don't worry, I'll always be a weirdo and a klutz and a friggin' Smurf. And I'll always do stupid shit, I'll always be having fun, I'll always be rocking guidette status, and I'll always be me. And I'll always be *tan*!

As for what's next, fricken bring it! One thing I know, my fans and fellow guidettes are the best. Always do you, and rock it! I love you, bitches!

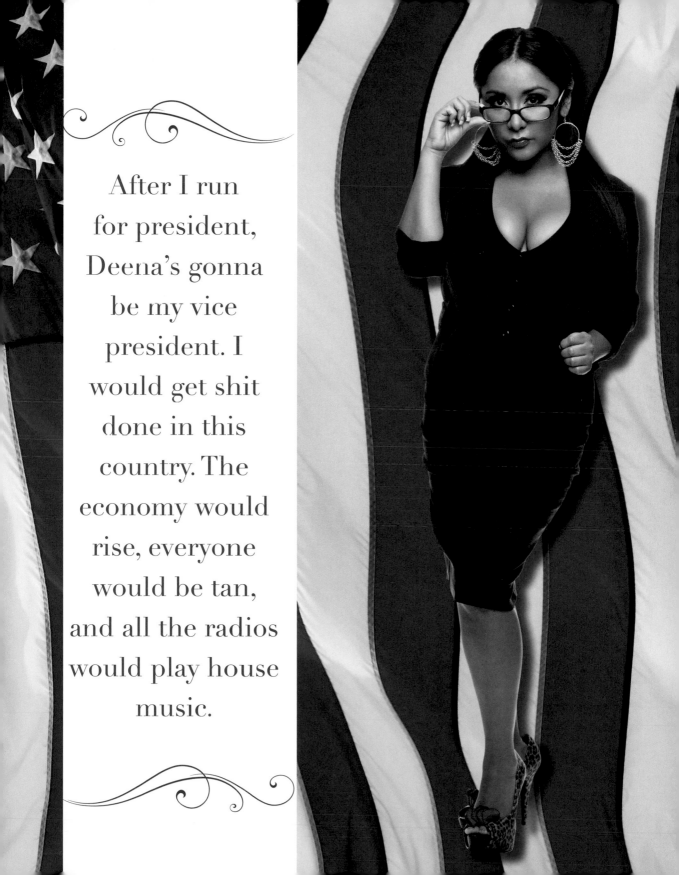

After I run for president, Deena's gonna be my vice president. I would get shit done in this country. The economy would rise, everyone would be tan, and all the radios would play house music.

PHOTO CREDITS

All stock background images and patterns are from istockphoto.com, with the exception of the gorilla on page 122, which is from shutterstock.com. Photos not listed below were provided by Nicole or her family from their private collections. (L = Left, R = Right)

Page ii, xiv, 175: Scott McDermott

Introduction: Page xii: Dimitrios Kambouris/WireImage

Chapter 1: Page 2: NY Post/Splash News ✻ Page 7: (*Bottom, L*) Jim Spellman/WireImage/Getty Images; (*Bottom, R*) Soul Brother/Film Magic/Getty Images; ✻ Page 8: Scott McDermott ✻ Page 13: Ernesto Ruscio/Getty Images/Getty Images

Chapter 2: Page 14: Scott McDermott ✻ Page 17: (*Middle, L*) John Parra/WireImage/Getty Images; (*Bottom, L*) Noel Vasquez/Getty Images/Getty Images; (*Bottom, R*) Matt Frisbie/Matt Frisbie Photography ✻ Page 18: (*Top, 2nd from R*) Jean Baptiste Lacroix/WireImage/Getty Images ✻ Page 24: Bobby Bank/WireImage/Getty Images ✻ Page 25: Vallery Jean/Getty Images/Getty Images ✻ Page 26: (*Top, L*) Photo © 2011 WWE. All Rights Reserved; (*2nd from L*) Janet Mayer/Splash News; (*Top, R*) Noel Vasquez/Getty Images/Getty Images; (*Bottom, L*) Alison Buck/WireImage/Getty Images; (*Bottom, Middle*) Jeff Kravitz/FilmMagic/Getty Images ✻ Page 27: (*Top, L*) Soul Brother/Getty Images/Getty Images; (*Top, R*) Denise Truscello/WireImage/Getty Images ✻ Page 28: (*Top, L*) John W. Ferguson/Getty Images/Getty Images; (*Top, 2nd from R*) Andy Kropa/Getty Images/Getty Images; (*Middle, L*) Christopher Peterson/ BuzzFoto/FilmMagic/Getty Images; (*Middle, Middle*) Janet Mayer/Splash News ✻ Page 29: (*Top, 2nd from R*) Bobby Bank/WireImage/Getty Images; (*Middle, R*) Dave Kotinsky/Getty Images/Getty Images; (*Bottom, L*) John Parra/WireImage/Getty Images; (*Bottom, R*) Dave Kotinsky/Getty Images/Getty Images ✻ Page 30: (*Bottom*) Soul Brother/FilmMagic/Getty Images ✻ Page 31: (*Top, L*) Andrew H. Walker/Getty Images; (*Top, Middle*) Ray Tamarra/Getty Images/Getty Images; (*Top, R*) Jean Baptiste Lacroix/WireImage/Getty Images; (*Middle*) Denise Truscello/WireImage/Getty Images; (*Bottom, L*) Andrew Rocke/Splash News; (*Bottom, Middle*) Andrew H. Walker/Getty Images; (*Bottom, R*) Bennett Raglin/WireImage/Getty Images ✻ Page 32: (*Top, L*) Jason Merritt/Getty Images/Getty Images; (*Top, 2nd from L*) Jason LaVeris/FilmMagic/Getty Images; (*Top, 2nd from R*) Jason LaVeris/FilmMagic/Getty Images; (*Top, R*) Andy Kropa/Getty Images/Getty Images; (*Bottom*) Andrew Rocke/Splash News ✻ Page 33: (*Top*) James Devaney/WireImage/Getty Images; (*Bottom, L*) James Devaney/WireImage/Getty Images; (*Bottom, Middle*) Christopher Peterson/ BuzzFoto/FilmMagic/Getty Images; (*Bottom, R*) James Devaney/WireImage/Getty Images ✻ Page 34: (L) John Parra/WireImages/Getty Images; (*Middle*) Dave Kotinsky/Getty Images/Getty Images; (R) Luca Ghidoni/FilmMagic/Getty Images ✻ Page 35: (L) Andrew H. Walker/Getty Images/Getty Images; (*2nd from L*) Jim Spellman/WireImage/Getty Images; (*2nd from R*) Vallery Jean/Getty Images/Getty Images; (R) Denise Truscello/WireImage/Getty Images ✻ Page 36: (L) Jason LaVeris/FilmMagic/Getty Images ✻ Page 37: (L) Matt Frisbie/Matt Frisbie Photography; (R) Janet Mayer/Splash News ✻ Page 38: (*Top, L*) Jon Kopaloff/FilmMagic/Getty Images; (*Top, R*) Frederick M. Brown/Getty Images/Getty Images; (*Middle, L*) Jason Merritt/Getty Images/Getty Images; (*Middle, R*) Dan MacMedan/WireImage/Getty Images; (*Bottom*) Taylor Hill/Getty Images/Getty Images ✻ Page 39: (*Top, L*) Kevin Mazur/WireImage/Getty Images; (*Top, R*) Jason Merritt/Getty Images/Getty Images; (*Far R*) Steven Lawton/FilmMagic/Getty Images

Chapter 3: Page 40: Scott McDermott ✻ Page 44: James Devaney/WireImage/Getty Images ✻ Page 46: (*Top*) PMM/FilmMagic/Getty Images; (*Bottom*) Christopher Peterson/BuzzFoto-FilmMagic/Getty Images ✻ Page 47: Steven Lawton/FilmMagic/Getty Images ✻ Page 51: Courtesy of Bryan Monti ✻

Page 52: (*Far R*) Elisabetta Villa/Getty Images ✱ Page 53: (*Middle*) Dave Kotinsky/Getty Images ✱ Page 54: Jean Baptiste Lacroix/WireImage/Getty Images ✱ Page 55: Luca Ghidoni/FilmMagic/Getty Images ✱ Page 57: Mike Coppola/Getty Images/Getty Images ✱ Page 61: Scott McDermott

Chapter 4: Page 62: Scott McDermott ✱ Page 65: John Parra/WireImage/Getty Images ✱ Page 67: Elisabetta Villa/Getty Images/Getty Images ✱ Page 69: Christopher Peterson/BuzzFoto-FilmMagic/Getty Images ✱ Page 70: (*Top*) John Parra/WireImage/Getty Images; (*Bottom, L*) Olivia Salazar/Getty Images/Getty Images; (*Bottom, R*) Larry Marano/FilmMagic/Getty Images ✱ Page 71: (*Top, L*) Dave Kotinsky/Getty Images/Getty Images; (*Top R*) Luca Ghidoni/FilmMagic/Getty Images; (*Bottom*) Brian Prahl/Splash News ✱ Page 72: Larry Marano/FilmMagic/Getty Images ✱ Page 73: Dave Kotinsky/Getty Images/Getty Images ✱ Page 75: NY Post/Splash News ✱ Page 76: Elisabetta Villa/Getty Images ✱ Page 77: (*Top*) Frederick M. Brown/Getty Images/Getty Images; (*Middle*) Jason Kempin/Getty Images/Getty Images; (*Bottom*) Mike Coppola/FilmMagic/Getty Images ✱ Page 81: (*Top*) Andrew H. Walker/Getty Images ✱ Page 82: (*Top*) Theo Wargo/Getty Images/Getty Images ✱ Page 83: Michael Caulfield/Getty Images/Getty Images ✱ Page 84: (*L*) Andrew H. Walker/Getty Images; (*R*) Kevin Mazur/WireImage/Getty Images ✱ Page 85: (*Top*) Courtesy of Danny Mackey; (*Bottom*) John W. Ferguson

Chapter 5: Page 88: Scott McDermott ✱ Page 91: Troy Rizzo/Getty Images/Getty Images ✱ Page 93: Christopher Peterson/BuzzFoto-FilmMagic/Getty Images ✱ Page 94: Jean Baptiste Lacroix/WireImage/Getty Images ✱ Page 95: Denise Truscello/WireImage/Getty Images ✱ Page 96: TS/Splash News ✱ Page 97: (*Bottom*) Larry Marano/Getty Images/Getty Images

Chapter 6: Page 102: Scott McDermott ✱ Page 110: Denise Truscello/WireImage/Getty Images ✱ Page 111: Denise Truscello/WireImage/Getty Images ✱ Page 113: (*Top, L*) Steve Mack/WireImage/Getty Images; (*Top, R*) Mr O/Splash News; (*R, Middle*) Mike Moore/WireImage/Getty Images; (*Bottom, L*) Kevin Mazur/WireImage/Getty Images; (*Bottom R*) Photo © 2011 WWE. All Rights Reserved ✱ Page 114: (*Top, L*) Joe Kohen/WireImage/Getty Images; (*Top, Middle*) Joe Kohen/WireImage/Getty Images; (*Top, R*) Jason Merritt/Getty Images ✱ Page 115: (*Middle*) Jerritt Clark/WireImage/Getty Images; (*Bottom*) Marc Stamas/Getty Images/Getty Images ✱ Page 116: (*Middle*) Steve Mack/FilmMagic/Getty Images ✱ Page 117: (*Top*) Photo © 2011 WWE. All Rights Reserved; (*Bottom, R*) Photo © 2011 WWE. All Rights Reserved; (*Bottom, L*) Mike Coppola/Getty Images/Getty Images ✱ Page 118: Rick Diamond/Getty Images/Getty Images ✱ Page 120: Bobby Bank/WireImage/Getty Images (2)

Chapter 7: Page 122: Scott McDermott ✱ Page 124: (*Middle*) Fred Montana/Splash News ✱ Page 125: (*L*) Troy Rizzo/Getty Images/Getty Images; (*R*) George Pimentel/WireImage/Getty Images ✱ Page 128: John Parra/WireImage/Getty Images ✱ Page 129: Elisabetta Villa/Getty Images ✱ Page 131: Carlos Alvarez/Getty Images/Getty Images ✱ Page 132: Denise Truscello/WireImage/Getty Images

Chapter 8: Page 136: Scott McDermott ✱ Page 139: Christopher Peterson/BuzzFoto-FilmMagic/Getty Images ✱ Page 141: (*R*) Noel Vasquez/Getty Images/Getty Images ✱ Page 142: Scott McDermott ✱ Page 143: Dimitrios Kambouris/WireImage/Getty Images ✱ Page 144: (*L*) Larry Marano/Getty Images/Getty Images; (*R*) Vallery Jean/FilmMagic/Getty Images ✱ Page 147: Photo © 2011 WWE. All Rights Reserved (3); (*Top, R*) Moses Robinson/Getty Images/Getty Images ✱ Page 148: Al Pereira/WireImage/Getty Images

Chapter 9: Page 150: Scott McDermott ✱ Page 153: James Devaney/WireImage/Getty Images ✱ Page 157: (*Bottom*) Ryan T/ Brian P/Splash News ✱ Page 166: Matt Frisbie/Matt Frisbie Photography ✱ Page 168: Denise Truscello/WireImage/Getty Images ✱ Page 169: Scott McDermott ✱ Pages 172–173: Soul Brother/FilmMagic/Getty Images

Snoo
was ne